THE LITTLE GREEN BOOK OF NOTE INVESTING

A Practical Guide for Getting Started with Investing in Mortgage Notes

FRED MOSKOWITZ

Disclaimer

This publication is designed to provide educational information in regard to the subject matter covered. You should use the information in this book at your own risk. It is sold with the understanding that neither the author nor the publisher are engaged in rendering legal, tax, accounting, or other professional services. If legal advice or other expert assistance is required, the services of a competent professional person should be sought.

Some names and identifying details have been changed to protect the privacy of individuals.

Published by Take Note Publishing, LLC, Philadelphia, PA.

Paperback ISBN: 978-0-578-78998-9

This book is dedicated to my father,
who taught me the value of taking action.

TABLE OF CONTENTS

INTRODUCTION

You are capable of remarkable things that you could never foretell and will never discover without taking action.

—Brendon Burchard, author and high-performance coach

MY STORY

I grew up learning about and following the traditional life model that we have often been told is best: go to school; get good grades; get a safe, secure job; work hard; and save money.

Although I grew up with entrepreneur's blood running through my veins, I suppressed those desires and right away began following the traditional model.

When I started working as an engineer after college, it did not take very long for me to realize that my career path was full of instability and adversity at the companies where I was employed, and even worse, in the grand scheme of things, I truly had very little control over its outcome. It was quite discouraging to arrive at the harsh realization that no matter how good of an employee I was, no matter how successful I was in my role, if business was not good at the company, I would be let go and lose my job.

I quickly gravitated to working for a tech start-up in the late 1990s, which was a very exciting time in the technology sector. We were focused on intense work, had heavy travel schedules, and were realizing many professional successes and accomplishments. My position was focused on traveling all over Latin America, successfully getting internet technology products deployed to the consumer markets at a time when the internet was starting to become widely accessible on a massive scale. Although I thoroughly enjoyed this work, after several years, I started to become burned out from the heavy travel and intense work schedules. As we approached the dot-com bust in the early 2000s, I began to see warning signs that the company was not doing well financially and that it was headed down the path of financial decline, eventually destined to go out of business. Being cautious, I began to save money to build up my cash reserves and prepare for what was to come.

As I watched the job market in the technology sectors begin to rapidly decline, the dot-com bust was getting into full swing with constant news about established technology companies that were closing or going bankrupt every week. I decided that it would be beneficial for me to take some time off, and I started to warm up to the idea of getting outside of my familiar and comfortable environment. My plan was that I would take an extended trip to Brazil, live near the beach, and study bossa nova guitar music for a while. I had saved enough to fund a nice sabbatical. I was a young single guy with no one else depending on me. Thinking about this started to get very exciting! I could close up my house and set up all my bills on electronic payment over the internet. This way, I could remotely manage my life from anywhere on the planet. This would provide me with a much-needed break from my hectic lifestyle and allow me to think about what my next career move would be. A number of years later when Tim Ferriss published his widely successful book *The 4-Hour Workweek*, he devoted an entire chapter to this same concept, which he called "mini retirements."

I went to Brazil with the intention of spending the summer there; however, due to several factors, I ended up extending my stay for a full year. The job market in the technology sector for engineers back home in the United States remained very poor, and there was also a major currency devaluation in Brazil, which meant that my US dollars would stretch significantly further. This allowed me to live a spartan but very comfortable life while spending very little of my savings. Taking these factors into consideration, I was in absolutely no hurry to return home, and I quickly began to like the idea of potentially skipping an entire winter in the northeastern United States.

During the time I was living in Brazil, I started to think about real estate and that I have seen firsthand how it could build significant wealth for those who went into it for a long-term play. I thought about the apartment that I had rented from George, who was my landlord while I was in college, and about how he was able to acquire a significant portfolio of rental real estate located within a couple of blocks of where we lived, all of which was rented out to students, and all the properties were owned without any debt (they were completely free and clear of mortgages). He achieved this with a lot of work over a very long time. I then decided right on the spot that when I got back home, I would start to look at buying an apartment building and learning how to manage and operate it effectively. I knew that I wanted to keep going in my career as an engineer but that I also wanted to start building my own streams of income to be able to replace my job income. I also came to the realization that in my work and my engineering career, I had been spending an inordinate amount of time basically building someone else's dream and not really building my own.

When I returned to Philadelphia, I truly came back a changed person. What I had found was that the disruptive act of ejecting yourself completely outside of your familiar and comfortable environment for any period of time will go a long way toward facilitating the clearing of your mind, making large decisions, and gaining clarity on your goals. This is the mindset that will allow you to begin to create massive change.

Now that I was back home, I reached out to some contacts who were working in real estate and mentioned that I was interested in starting to invest and in purchasing an apartment building. The first suggestions and recommendations I received were to read Robert Kiyosaki's book *Rich Dad Poor Dad*, and also to join the local Real Estate Investors Association (REIA) in my city. After reading that book and then attending my first REIA meeting, where I was suddenly around hundreds of successful investors, I immediately knew I was headed on the right path and confirmed that this was what I wanted to pursue. I pushed forward, and within a few months I acquired my first property, which was a four-unit apartment building. Three months later I purchased a second property, and then continued on an aggressive acquisition streak, never looking back. Each time I purchased a property, I worked quickly to get it renovated or repositioned and to place a tenant, and then I began to search for the next property. Since the credit markets were very loose during this time period, I continued acquiring for several years. I always purchased real estate using solid investment fundamentals, namely, buying property for cash flow and not for speculation, with good financing in place, which left me very well positioned during the downturn that came in 2007.

My involvement in my local REIA afforded me the opportunity to attend educational seminars and events with many high-level real estate professionals that were at the top of their game. It was in attending educational workshops taught by master real estate educators Peter Fortunato and Jack Miller that I first heard about the concept of notes as an investment; however, this was in the context of buying or selling an investment property. The concept was about the seller offering financing to the buyer as part of the transaction (also known as carrying back seller financing), thereby originating your own note. The term *originating a note* means "to create the note," effectively becoming a lender. In doing this, you could sell a property but then continue to earn monthly cash flow for many years after the sale.

The idea sounded interesting and appealing. However, as I was in a focused property-acquisition mode at the time, the furthest thought from my mind was to entertain selling one of my properties.

Sometime later, I attended a workshop presented by Jimmy Napier (author of the book *Invest In Debt*), and the workshop was on the topic of negotiating. As often is the case when attending these workshops, some of the best golden nuggets show up out of the side remarks and discussions when the presenter gets off track from the topic of the event. Jimmy went on to tell us about one of his businesses, which was involved in lending money locally in his town. He explained to us how real estate was an excellent vehicle in which to build capital for a young person who was just starting out, due to the leverage involved. However, for those investors in it for the long game, there was a huge advantage to eventually taking some of that capital off the table and reinvesting it into debt investments, which would allow you to grow the capital at a significantly much higher rate than if it had been left invested in the real estate.

That idea remained firmly planted in my mind for several years until I had the opportunity to take action by learning in detail about note investing and getting started with buying my first couple of notes.

HOW THIS BOOK WILL BENEFIT YOU

> Formal education will make you a living; self-education will make you a fortune.
>
> —Jim Rohn, author and motivational speaker

My goal with this book is to inspire you to get involved with note investing, whether you do so in an active or a passive role. This will empower you to improve your financial future by putting your hard-earned dollars to work for you. Remember, if you are working at a job in your profession, although it may be rewarding to you, you are always trading time for dollars. When you stop trading your time, the dollars will also stop coming in. If a major event happens in your life and you need to stop working for an extended amount of time, that income will come to a grinding halt. Has that ever happened to you or to someone you know? Hopefully there was a rainy-day fund in place to cover the bills until you were able to go back to work.

However, if you are earning passive income with your money working for you, that recurring income will continue to come in no matter what is happening in your own life. This will provide tremendous stability for those times where you are not able to work, such as:

- Temporary job loss or corporate downsizing
- Medical or health issues
- Maternity/paternity leave (fully enjoying the experience of welcoming a newborn child into your life)
- Caring for a sick family member

Note investing is a very powerful way to generate passive income on a recurring basis. This business is not just for the financial institutions and the hedge funds on Wall Street. The note business is also on Main Street and accessible to individual investors such as yourself!

Are you in the note business now? You probably are, and you don't even know it.

Consider that if you are making payments on any of the following financial obligations, then, yes, you are in the note business!

- Student loans
- Auto loans
- Home mortgage
- Personal bank loans
- Credit cards
- Equipment financing
- Business loans

The problem is that you are on the wrong side of the note business. How would you like to step across that aisle into the shoes of the lender and be the recipient of those monthly payments? With note investing, this is exactly what you are doing. In this book, we will be exploring the exciting world of note investing and learning how to evaluate, purchase, and invest in notes.

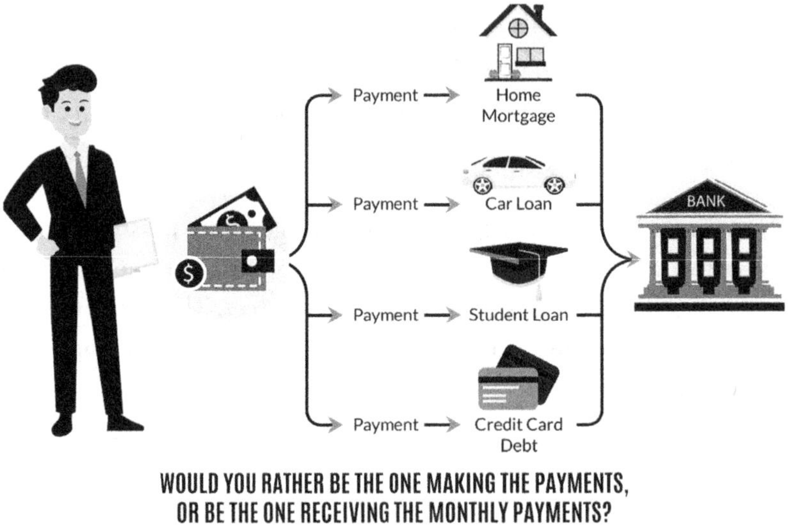

FIGURE 0.1. THE NOTE BUSINESS AT A GLANCE

Financial literacy and the understanding of how debt works are not topics that are taught to us in our school system. This puts the public at large at a tremendous disadvantage, and many people are at risk of being taken advantage of financially.

Those who are comfortable to depend solely on the government (relying only on 401(k) plans and/or Social Security) to provide income in their later years of life potentially could be facing some serious surprises and disappointments.

About a decade ago, I made a major decision to educate myself and get started with note investing, and to establish my business of buying mortgages at discounts and then holding them for long-term cash flow. By writing this book, my goal is to educate and empower you, the reader, to learn how to leverage the power of note investing to help achieve your dreams and goals in life. Empowered with that knowledge, you will be able to live at your highest potential.

401(k) Plans—Don't Let Wall Street Fool You into Overpaying for Underperformance

I'd like to share a story with you. I was recently speaking with a friend about investment results for the year. He was telling me about his financial advisor, who was managing funds for him. This advisor was able to get him a 4% return for the past five years. However, as we dug into the details, there were fees to the advisor of 2.5%, inflation of 2%, and the net result was that he lost money at the end of the period. Now that's what I call overpaying for underperformance!

I have experienced similar results with my own 401(k) account when I was working as an engineer in the technology sector. I recall at one particular end of year, I was going back and looking at my 401(k) statements for the previous twelve months. I knew that the stock market had done moderately well over the past year, but for some reason, my year-over-year account balance had only increased just about the same amount as my annual contribution plus the employer matching.

I said, "What happened to the return on all the funds invested?"

I put a pencil to the numbers and dug into some of the finer details, and I noticed that a pattern had started to emerge.

Each year, there would be a modest return from the stock market, from which would be subtracted fees for the 401(k) administrator, then fees for each mutual fund in which I was invested, and then inflation. This would completely erode any gains for the year, and my 401(k) account ultimately increased in value pretty much by the same amount that I had contributed for the year. And that was just for the years that the stock market did OK and returned its "average" returns. Sound familiar?

In the years where the stock market had a down year, the account would decrease in value, compounded by the fees still being paid out, resulting in an even greater loss. Doesn't that pain hurt twice as much?

Now, I completely understand that fees need to be charged by companies and institutions that are in business to provide a service. However, I feel that there needs to be clear transparency of all fees that are being charged to consumers so that we, as consumers, are able to make well-informed investment decisions. The bottom line is that 401(k) administrators make it very hard to find fees. For the customer who is searching for them, it gets very frustrating! There is not a 401(k) administrator out there who will send you a bill at the end of the year that details how much you were charged for them managing your retirement funds. As a result, this information gets handled with a "don't ask, don't tell" type of policy. Remember that as long as the employees are not asking about these fees, the administrators are not talking about the expenses. **You may visit www.fredmoskowitz.com/401k to receive a special report about how to calculate the fees in your 401(k) plan.**

I encourage you to consider note investing as a strategy that you can utilize to augment your existing investments. Since the performance of the asset class of notes and mortgages is not correlated to the stock market, this asset class helps to provide a level of counterbalance and stability to your overall portfolio. For those periods when the financial gains from Wall Street investments are dwindling, having a portion of your capital invested in solid assets that generate consistent income will provide a significant boost to your overall returns and a very welcome peace of mind.

KEY CONCEPTS

You, as the reader, have a choice. You can choose to keep doing as so many people do, which is living paycheck to paycheck, perpetually stuck in a financial rut and feeling helpless about not being able to change your financial situation. Or you can set the intention to learn and understand the financial concepts presented in this book, and then, most importantly, take action and actually implement what you have learned. Remember that you are ultimately responsible for your financial future. I hope you choose the latter, and I welcome you on this journey together with me!

In the coming chapters, we will explore the following concepts of note investing:

- The benefits of diversification into alternative investments and how to include the asset class of notes as part of that diversification
- The concept of buying a note at a discount and the impact of that discount on your rate of return
- The evaluation of a note and how to perform due diligence before making an offer to purchase
- The mechanics of a note purchase transaction
- Boarding the note and the loan servicing transfer
- Risk management
- Note sourcing
- Buying notes in your retirement account and an overview on self-directed retirement accounts
- Investing in note partials
- Investing in note funds
- Using debt you own to pay for debt you incur

1

WHY DOES NOTE INVESTING DESERVE A PLACE IN YOUR OVERALL INVESTMENT PORTFOLIO?

I am a firm believer in long-term income streams.

—Jimmy Napier, author and real estate educator

ASSET CLASSES—CONVENTIONAL INVESTMENTS AND ALTERNATIVE INVESTMENTS

Most people are quite familiar with the conventional investment categories that are the Wall Street–related investments: stocks, bonds, and mutual funds. These categories are what are most often discussed in the mainstream media, and these are what are made available in most employer 401(k) plans.

Alternative investments are assets that do not fit into one of the conventional investment buckets. These include private equity, business ownership, or direct investing into businesses, real estate, precious metals, and notes. Alternative investments, in most cases, have little or no correlation to the stock market. Fairly often, we will observe that the value of alternative investments does not move very much during times of turbulence in the stock market. This is a very significant benefit, and therefore, alternative investments can provide an effective measure for very good investment portfolio diversification.

Investing in notes is certainly considered an alternative investment. In my speaking and meeting with thousands of investors over the years, I often encounter people who are looking for options for diversification and alternative investment opportunities. There is tremendous opportunity out there for all of us, and all it takes is dedication and effort to pursue education and networking with the right people.

STEPPING OVER TO THE OTHER SIDE OF THE AISLE AND BECOMING THE BANK

Note investing affords the opportunity for individual investors to step into the shoes of the lender and become the bank. If you have any experience with lending or originating loans, you know how much work is involved with originating the loan, qualifying the borrower, and staying in compliance with federal and state lending regulations. Many investors I know like to originate what are called "hard money loans," or private lending, where they are lending at high interest rates to local real estate investors for short-term development projects. Typically these are commercial loans to quickly buy and renovate properties for profit, the loans are in place for six to twelve months, and then they are paid off when the property is sold or refinanced with more traditional long-term financing. Something to keep in mind with this is that because the capital keeps coming back to the lender within one year, the lender has to be constantly seeking out new projects and borrowers for which to redeploy their capital in order to keep the capital working for them. Any amount of time that capital is returned (due to a loan payoff) and sits idle creates a negative drag effect on the lender's overall rate of return.

The focus of this book is on investing in performing notes that have already been originated and have some sort of a track record on the payment history (also called "seasoning"). Keeping in mind that the average life span of a home mortgage in the United States is five to seven years before a property is either sold or refinanced, mortgage notes provide us with a longer time frame in which to generate our investment returns. Also, when we purchase a note at a discount to what is owed, when the time comes for the loan to pay off, there will be a spread between the discounted purchase price of the note and the payoff amount. This additional profit can provide a very strong boost to the overall rate of return for the note investment.

Here's a quick example to illustrate this concept (which is sometimes referred to in the note industry as a "kicker"). A note with a principal balance of $100,000 is purchased by an investor at a discount for $85,000. Let's suppose that the following month, the property is sold, and the note is paid off in full for $100,000. The investor then will receive the full payoff amount, consisting of her $85,000 initial investment, plus the $15,000, which is pure profit.

One thing you may have noticed is that banks are not in the business of being landowners. Instead, they are in the business of being lien holders. Banks figured out hundreds of years ago that they are able to originate and hold notes on hundreds and thousands of properties with relative ease to scale up in very large numbers of assets. If you are currently a real estate investor, I would like you to consider your own rental portfolio. Perhaps you currently own one, ten, twenty-five, fifty, or even one hundred rental properties. What would it take, and what kind of life would you have, if you were to scale the amount of properties that you own by ten times? Maybe you could successfully pull this off, but what quality of life would you have? What would be the impact to your health and to the stability of your family?

When investing in notes, it is possible to massively scale and to continue scaling your business. Note servicers play a pivotal role in this concept of scaling. Think of a note servicer as a property manager for a note. The role of a note servicer is to take on the responsibility for collecting the payments, handling the accounting and amortization schedule on the loan (for both the borrower and the lender), sending out any necessary compliance letters to borrowers, fielding telephone calls from the borrowers, handling collection activities when needed, coordinating payoffs with title and escrow agents, and releasing the lien when the loan is paid off. Owning a large note portfolio containing tens, hundreds, or even thousands of notes becomes a very realistic possibility when we leverage the services and expertise of a loan servicer.

Another detail about note investing that will resonate with those of you who own rentals is dealing with the mindset of a homeowner as opposed to the mindset of a tenant. When there is a leaking roof, broken heater, electrical problem, or other maintenance issue in a house, does a homeowner ever call the bank or lender to ask to have the problem fixed?

By all means, investing in rental real estate and holding it long term offers tremendous benefits, and it does have a place in your portfolio; however, remember that there are limitations on how that can be scaled.

I would like for you to consider the idea of owning debt as part of your overall investment portfolio, especially during the late part of an economic cycle. With performing notes that have a solid track record, the stability and predictability of your investment outcome is significantly increased. Additionally, there is a significant noncorrelation to the overall stock market conditions.

Note investing is largely a learning-by-doing activity. Yes, it is important to have a good education and solid guidance. I encourage you to get involved and get started with your investing, either actively or passively. Do not sit on the sidelines and be a spectator. If you stay in this business for the long game, you will be rewarded as you watch your slow, steady growth over time!

GETTING PAID WHILE YOU WAIT!

I was introduced to Samantha by a mutual friend at an educational investment conference. Samantha, a married mother of two children, was working very hard to help support her household. She was very accomplished in her career as a pharmaceutical sales professional, and being in her fifties, she often found herself questioning the effectiveness of her retirement planning, which consisted of her employer 401(k) plan along with some stock market investments and some IRAs from prior employers. Her husband, who also worked for a company in the same industry, also contributed similarly to his employer's retirement plan. Samantha felt that their progress in saving for retirement was rather lackluster despite the fact that they had been diligently saving and investing in their retirement accounts for the previous twenty-five years. Samantha was plagued with the uncertainty of being able to retire on time after sacrificing and working very hard for decades. You see, during the previous market downturn they watched years of steady gains get wiped out almost overnight. Samantha remembers that day when she got into her car to head home after a long day of making sales calls, and she turned on the radio to hear the news of another major stock market crash. She felt a pit deep in her stomach as she drove home and anxiously logged in to check her retirement account balance online. As she looked at the statement flash up on the screen, she felt filled with anguish as she asked herself, "How will we ever put our children through college and retire with all these wild market swings?"

Samantha decided in that moment that they had to make major changes in their investment plan, and she turned to alternative investments. She started attending investment-related events where she could learn and also put herself around other successful investors that were active with alternative investments not tied to the stock market. She set a goal for her and her husband to earn $5,000 per month from passive investments that generate cash flow. After meeting and talking to some very successful investors, quite a lot of them seemed to come back to the strategy of investing in performing notes. Not knowing anything about note investing, she decided to seek out people that were successful in notes and learn from them. Some of the investors were sophisticated and had implemented elaborate investment strategies that were way over her head, however performing notes seemed to be a strategy that really resonated with her. It was very straightforward and easy for her to understand, and before you knew it, she had purchased her first couple of notes and was soon earning monthly cash flow.

Samantha was also able to take note of new opportunities by building relationships with top-class investment operators, and she ended up participating in several deals as a passive investor—apartment syndications, a commercial real estate deal, and a note fund. The combination of these assets allowed her to significantly grow those retirement accounts while generating recurring cash flow. Samantha was very pleased with the concept of "*getting paid while you wait,*" and felt a tremendous weight lifted from her shoulders upon seeing firsthand the direct impact it had on her financial goals. She and her husband absolutely loved receiving the email notifications of electronic payments that were being deposited in their accounts each month. Those days of feeling anxiety and worry about retirement were now but distant memories from her past.

KEY CONCEPTS

- Alternative investments are typically investments that are not Wall Street–related, such as real estate, private businesses, funding a start-up company, notes, and mortgages. They have little or no correlation to the stock market.
- Note investing allows investors to step into the shoes of the bank and to become the one receiving the monthly payments, earning a superior rate of return.
- Notes are typically sold at a discount with respect to the amount of the debt, which in turn drives up the rate of return proportionally to the discount.
- Banks are in the business of being lien holders instead of landowners. Understand the benefits of following their lead.

2

THE BASICS

WHAT IS NOTE INVESTING?
HOW CAN YOU GET INVOLVED IN NOTE INVESTING?

Invest in as much of yourself as you can,
you are your own biggest asset by far.

—Warren Buffett, investor and philanthropist

WHAT IS NOTE INVESTING?

Most people do not know that they can become the bank. Instead, we are subject to a stream of constant marketing and advertising from financial investment companies that want you to invest in their offerings such as stocks, bonds, and mutual funds. There is a major industry around the marketing and selling of these financial products, with commissions tied to each transaction. However, there are alternatives available to us. With note investing, a person is able to buy a note, and to effectively become the bank.

A note, or a promissory note, is a legal instrument that contains a written promise to pay a sum of money to the bearer of the document. This note is then secured by a security instrument, known as a mortgage. This security instrument is what ties the debt to the deed as a lien against the property (an encumbrance) as collateral backing the note.

When an investor purchases the note and its security interest, the mortgage, then that investor has purchased the secured debt and effectively becomes the bank. We can think about the analogy of the way that a personal check can be endorsed over to a new payee. With this same concept, a note and mortgage can also be endorsed or assigned over to a new payee.

The new owner of the secured debt has the right to receive the outstanding loan payments along with all the benefits and protections, which are spelled out in the note and mortgage documents. The investor will now receive the stream of recurring payments as passive income for the remaining term of the note.

A mortgage loan is what facilitates the buyer of a property to obtain financing in order to purchase a property, and that property is pledged as collateral in order to guarantee the loan. This type of transaction is well established and has been in existence for hundreds of years. When someone purchases a house or commercial property with financing, they will put a down payment toward the purchase price of the property and finance the remaining balance with a mortgage loan, most often with a repayment term of fifteen, twenty, or thirty years.

When you hear the term "investing in a note," this refers to someone who is purchasing and, therefore, investing in the debt. It is the acquisition of a payment stream or cash flow for the purpose of earning a rate of return—a profit—on the invested dollars. Investing in a note, in most cases, is defined as investing in a mortgage loan. The mortgage loan is purchased by the investor, typically at a discount to the amount owed. The mortgage loan consists of two primary instruments: the note and the mortgage. Let's explore the characteristics of these instruments.

THE NOTE

This is a promissory note (a promise to pay), and it is a contractual document that outlines the financial terms of the loan, such as interest rate, payment amount, and term for repayment. The note is a private agreement between the borrower and the lender and is not customarily part of the public record.

THE MORTGAGE

Also called "the deed of trust" in most of the western United States, this document, when signed by the borrower, is what gives the lender a security interest in the property. The mortgage document is recorded in the county courthouse where the property is located and becomes part of the public record. By recording the mortgage or deed of trust in the public record, the general public is put on notice that there is a lien or encumbrance registered against the property. This security interest protects the lender in the case of a loan default or a sale of the property. In the case of a default, the mortgage is what will allow the lender to take the property back by the legal process of foreclosure. A title search of the public record that is run on the property will normally show all mortgages, liens, and other encumbrances against the property, and the lender will require each of these to be addressed during a subsequent sale or refinance of the property. When there are multiple mortgages or liens recorded against the same property, the position of each lien is established in an order based upon the date of recording. This gives us the concept in liens of first position, second position, third position, and so on.

There exists a vast secondary market for the buying and selling of debt of all types: residential and commercial mortgages, automobile debt, aviation debt, and equipment debt. (All are debts secured by the title to the asset in order to guarantee the loan.) Also, there are many types of unsecured debt, such as credit card debt, student (educational) loans, medical debt, and personal loans. In this book, we will be focusing on the most common type of mortgage debt, which is loans secured by residential property.

How does one get involved in note investing? Here are the main methods.

SELLER OR OWNER FINANCING

You can originate a note through seller financing, which is the process of selling a property you own to a buyer and, as part of the transaction, writing a note and a mortgage for the buyer. Instead of the financing for the property coming from a bank or mortgage company, the financing is coming from the seller of the property. This technique can be beneficial to both the buyer and seller in several situations:

- To facilitate the selling of a property that would not qualify for a traditional mortgage due to the property condition (such as a distressed property, a fire-damaged property, environmental issues, etc.) or the characteristics of the property (commercial property, mobile home park, church, farm, etc.)

- To facilitate the selling of a property to a buyer who is having trouble qualifying for bank financing (self-employed buyers, buyers with poor credit history, real estate investors with many loans in their name, etc.)
- To sell the property on an installment sale (reference the IRS publication 537 on installment sales), allowing the seller to spread out their tax liability from the sale of the property over multiple years, which is particularly beneficial to the seller when they are facing a major tax liability upon sale of the property. This often is the case when the property has been owned for a long period of time, and the property has both appreciated in value and has been fully depreciated for tax purposes.

PURCHASING A NOTE FROM A NOTE SELLER

The direct purchase and sale of an existing note from one individual or institution to another. There exists a secondary mortgage market where mortgage loans are bought and sold every day between lenders and investors. Keeping in mind that banks and lenders are in the business of originating loans, they will sell their loans (at a discount) in order to recapitalize, making money available to go back and originate additional loans.

CROWD-BASED LENDING PLATFORMS AND PEER-TO-PEER LENDING

There are online platforms that connect lenders directly to borrowers. These lending platforms allow investors to deploy their capital in small chunks (sometimes as little as twenty-five dollars) spread across many loans of similar characteristics. This capital is then used to originate loans for borrowers directly on the platform.

INVESTING IN NOTE FUNDS

With note funds, the fund manager raises capital from individual investors. That capital is then pooled together to acquire notes in volume and hold them for cash flow in order to generate income, according to the fund's operating model and business plan. Note funds are an excellent option for investors who are seeking a passive return on their capital, with the added benefit that they are able to leverage the experience, skills, expertise, and relationships of the fund manager. Investors who are busy professionals focused on their careers and businesses and do not have the time to dedicate to notes tend to find that participating in note funds is an excellent option for them. Note funds also offer investors the added benefit of spreading out their investment capital among many assets, resulting in a superior diversification and risk-management strategy.

BENEFITS OF OWNING AND HOLDING NOTES FOR THE LONG TERM

Owning and holding notes for the long term can provide significant benefits:

- You own an investment that is secured, or collateralized. The securing of a note happens when the mortgage is recorded at the county courthouse or county recorder's office in the county where the property is located, and this becomes part of the public record. If the property is ever sold or refinanced in the future, the title company handling the transfer will run a title search, in which the public record is researched to establish the full chain of title (all previous transfers of the property from one owner to the next) along with any unsatisfied liens and encumbrances recorded against the property. These liens and encumbrances will need to be satisfied in order for the property owner to be able to deliver, or convey, what is known as clear title of ownership to the new owner. If you are the holder of the mortgage, the title company will be contacting you to request a payoff quote for the lien in preparation for the sale of the property. In the case of a refinance, the new lender will typically require that prior liens be satisfied so that their lien will be in the appropriate lien position (usually first or second position), as was agreed in the terms of the financing.

- Notes are typically bought and sold at a discount. When notes are sold at a discount to what is owed, this results in an increased yield, or rate of return, for the note buyer. This rate of return becomes higher than the interest rate specified in the note, which is being paid by the borrower.
- Owning note investments over the long term can produce excellent cash flow and a high rate of return. Rates of return ranging between 8% and 16%, or even higher, are common.

How does an investor profit from notes? In two ways: cash flow and discount.

CASH FLOW

Note payments consist of principal and interest and are amortized according to the original terms of the note. An amortization schedule is a table that lists all the payments on a note over the time of the term. This amortization schedule details, for each payment, the amount allocated to interest and to principal.

In Figure 2.1, we show part of an amortization table for our example loan (a $100,000 loan with a thirty-year repayment term and 6% interest rate):

COMPOUNDING PERIOD: MONTHLY
NOMINAL ANNUAL RATE: 6.000%

$100,000 LOAN, 30 YEAR TERM, 6% INTEREST RATE - LOANS AND PAYMENTS

	EVENT	DATE	AMOUNT	NUMBER	PERIOD	END DATE
1	Loan	12/01/2019	100,000	1		
2	Payment	01/01/2020	599.55	360	Monthly	12/01/2049

AMORTIZATION SCHEDULE - NORMAL, 365 DAY YEAR

	DATE	PAYMENT	INTEREST	PRINCIPAL	BALANCE
Loan	12/01/2019				100,000,00
2019 TOTALS		**0.00**	**0.00**	**0.00**	
1	01/01/2020	599.55	500.00	99.55	99,900.45
2	02/01/2020	599.55	499.50	100.05	99,800.40
3	03/01/2020	599.55	499.00	100.55	99,699.85
4	04/01/2020	599.55	498.50	101.05	99,598.80
5	05/01/2020	599.55	497.99	101.56	99,497.24
6	06/01/2020	599.55	497.49	102.06	99,395.18
7	07/01/2020	599.55	496.98	102.57	99,292.61
8	08/01/2020	599.55	496.46	103.09	99,189.52
9	09/01/2020	599.55	495.95	103.60	99,085.92
10	10/01/2020	599.55	495.43	104.12	98,981.80
11	11/01/2020	599.55	494.91	104.64	98,877.16
12	12/01/2020	599.55	494.39	105.16	98,772.00

	DATE	PAYMENT	INTEREST	PRINCIPAL	BALANCE
2020 TOTALS		**7,194.60**	**5,966.60**	**1,228.00**	
13	01/01/2021	599.55	493.86	105.69	98,666.31
14	02/01/2021	599.55	493.33	106.22	98,560.09
15	03/01/2021	599.55	492.80	106.75	98,453.34
16	04/01/2021	599.55	492.27	107.28	98,346.06
17	05/01/2021	599.55	491.73	107.82	98,238.24
18	06/01/2021	599.55	491.19	108.36	98,129.88
19	07/01/2021	599.55	490.65	108.90	98,020.98
20	08/01/2021	599.55	490.10	109.45	97,911.53
21	09/01/2021	599.55	489.56	109.99	97,801.54
22	10/01/2021	599.55	489.01	110.54	97,691.00
23	11/01/2021	599.55	488.46	111.09	97,579.91
24	12/01/2021	599.55	487.90	111.65	97,468.26
2021 TOTALS		**7,194.60**	**5,890.86**	**1,303.74**	
25	01/01/2022	599.55	487.34	112.21	97,356.05
26	02/01/2022	599.55	486.78	112.77	97,243.28
27	03/01/2022	599.55	486.22	113.33	97,129.95
28	04/01/2022	599.55	485.65	113.90	97,016.05
29	05/01/2022	599.55	485.08	114.47	96,901.58
30	06/01/2022	599.55	484.51	115.04	96,786.54
31	07/01/2022	599.55	483.93	115.62	96,670.92
32	08/01/2022	599.55	483.35	116.20	96,554.72
33	09/01/2022	599.55	482.77	116.78	96,437.94
34	10/01/2022	599.55	482.19	117.36	96,320.58
35	11/01/2022	599.55	481.60	117.95	96,202.63
36	12/01/2022	599.55	481.01	118.54	96,084.09
2022 TOTALS		**7,194.60**	**5,810.43**	**1,384.17**	
37	01/01/2023	599.55	480.42	119.13	95,964.96
38	02/01/2023	599.55	479.82	119.73	95,845.23
39	03/01/2023	599.55	479.23	120.32	95,724.91
40	04/01/2023	599.55	478.62	120.93	95,603.98
41	05/01/2023	599.55	478.02	121.53	95,482.45
42	06/01/2023	599.55	477.41	122.14	95,360.31
43	07/01/2023	599.55	476.80	122.75	95,237.56
44	08/01/2023	599.55	476.19	123.36	95,114.20
45	09/01/2023	599.55	475.57	123.98	94,990.22
46	10/01/2023	599.55	474.95	124.60	94,865.62
47	11/01/2023	599.55	474.33	125.22	94,740.40
48	12/01/2023	599.55	473.70	125.85	94,614.55

	DATE	PAYMENT	INTEREST	PRINCIPAL	BALANCE
2023 TOTALS		7,194.60	5,725.06	1,469.54	
49	01/01/2024	599.55	473.07	126.48	94,488.07
50	02/01/2024	599.55	472.44	127.11	94,360.96
51	03/01/2024	599.55	471.80	127.75	94,233.21
52	04/01/2024	599.55	471.17	128.38	94,104.83
53	05/01/2024	599.55	470.52	129.03	93,975.80
54	06/01/2024	599.55	469.88	129.67	93,846.13
55	07/01/2024	599.55	469.23	130.32	93,715.81
56	08/01/2024	599.55	468.58	130.97	93,584.84
57	09/01/2024	599.55	467.92	131.63	93,453.21
58	10/01/2024	599.55	467.27	132.28	93,320.93
59	11/01/2024	599.55	466.60	132.95	93,187.98
60	12/01/2024	599.55	465.94	133.61	93,054.37
2024 TOTALS		**7,194.60**	**5,634.42**	**1,560.18**	
61	01/01/2025	599.55	465.27	134.28	92,920.09
62	02/01/2025	599.55	464.60	134.95	92,785.14
63	03/01/2025	599.55	463.93	135.62	92,649.52
64	04/01/2025	599.55	463.25	136.30	92,513.22
65	05/01/2025	599.55	462.57	136.98	92,376.24
66	06/01/2025	599.55	461.88	137.67	92,238.57
67	07/01/2025	599.55	461.19	138.36	92,100.21
68	08/01/2025	599.55	460.50	139.05	91,961.16
69	09/01/2025	599.55	459.81	139.74	91,821.42
70	10/01/2025	599.55	459.11	140.44	91,680.98
71	11/01/2025	599.55	458.40	141.15	91,539.83
72	12/01/2025	599.55	457.70	141.85	91,397.98
2025 TOTALS		**7,194.60**	**5,538.21**	**1,656.39**	
73	01/01/2026	599.55	456.99	142.56	91,255.42
74	02/01/2026	599.55	456.28	143.27	91,112.15
75	03/01/2026	599.55	455.56	143.99	90,968.16
76	04/01/2026	599.55	454.84	144.71	90,823.45
77	05/01/2026	599.55	454.12	145.43	90,678.02
78	06/01/2026	599.55	453.39	146.16	90,531.86
79	07/01/2026	599.55	452.66	146.89	90,384.97
80	08/01/2026	599.55	451.92	147.63	90,237.34
81	09/01/2026	599.55	451.19	148.36	90,088.98
82	10/01/2026	599.55	450.44	149.11	89,939.87
83	11/01/2026	599.55	449.70	149.85	89,790.02
84	12/01/2026	599.55	448.95	150.60	89,639.42

	DATE	PAYMENT	INTEREST	PRINCIPAL	BALANCE
2026 TOTALS		**7,194.60**	**5,436.04**	**1,758.56**	
85	01/01/2027	599.55	448.20	151.35	89,488.07
86	02/01/2027	599.55	447.44	152.11	89,335.96
87	03/01/2027	599.55	446.68	152.87	89,183.09
88	04/01/2027	599.55	445.92	153.63	89,029.46
89	05/01/2027	599.55	445.15	154.40	88,875.06
90	06/01/2027	599.55	444.38	155.17	88,719.89
91	07/01/2027	599.55	443.60	155.95	88,563.94
92	08/01/2027	599.55	442.82	156.73	88,407.21
93	09/01/2027	599.55	442.04	157.51	88,249.70
94	10/01/2027	599.55	441.25	158.30	88,091.40
95	11/01/2027	599.55	440.46	159.09	87,932.31
96	12/01/2027	599.55	439.66	159.89	87,772.42
2027 TOTALS		**7,194.60**	**5,327.60**	**1,867.00**	
97	01/01/2028	599.55	438.86	160.69	87,611.73
98	02/01/2028	599.55	438.06	161.49	87,450.24
99	03/01/2028	599.55	437.25	162.30	87,287.94
100	04/01/2028	599.55	436.44	163.11	87,124.83
101	05/01/2028	599.55	435.62	163.93	86,960.90
102	06/01/2028	599.55	434.80	164.75	86,796.15
103	07/01/2028	599.55	433.98	165.57	86,630.58
104	08/01/2028	599.55	433.15	166.40	86,464.18
105	09/01/2028	599.55	432.32	167.23	86,296.95
106	10/01/2028	599.55	431.48	168.07	86,128.88
107	11/01/2028	599.55	430.64	168.91	85,959.97
108	12/01/2028	599.55	429.80	169.75	85,790.22
2028 TOTALS		**7,194.60**	**5,212.40**	**1,982.20**	
109	01/01/2029	599.55	428.95	170.60	85,619.62
110	02/01/2029	599.55	428.10	171.45	85,448.17
111	03/01/2029	599.55	427.24	172.31	85,275.86
112	04/01/2029	599.55	426.38	173.17	85,102.69
113	05/01/2029	599.55	425.51	174.04	84,928.65
114	06/01/2029	599.55	424.64	174.91	84,753.74
115	07/01/2029	599.55	423.77	175.78	84,577.96
116	08/01/2029	599.55	422.89	176.66	84,401.30
117	09/01/2029	599.55	422.01	177.54	84,223.76
118	10/01/2029	599.55	421.12	178.43	84,045.33
119	11/01/2029	599.55	420.23	179.32	83,866.01
120	12/01/2029	599.55	419.33	180.22	83,685.79

	DATE	PAYMENT	INTEREST	PRINCIPAL	BALANCE
2029 TOTALS		**7,194.60**	**5,090.17**	**2,104.43**	
121	01/01/2030	599.55	418.43	181.12	83,504.67
122	02/01/2030	599.55	417.52	182.03	83,322.64
123	03/01/2030	599.55	416.61	182.94	83,139.70
124	04/01/2030	599.55	415.70	183.85	82,955.85
125	05/01/2030	599.55	414.78	184.77	82,771.08
126	06/01/2030	599.55	413.86	185.69	82,585.39
127	07/01/2030	599.55	412.93	186.62	82,398.77
128	08/01/2030	599.55	411.99	187.56	82,211.21
129	09/01/2030	599.55	411.06	188.49	82,022.72
130	10/01/2030	599.55	410.11	189.44	81,833.28
131	11/01/2030	599.55	409.17	190.38	81,642.90
132	12/01/2030	599.55	408.21	191.34	81,451.56
2030 TOTALS		**7,194.60**	**4,960.37**	**2,234.23**	
133	01/01/2031	599.55	407.26	192.29	81,259.27
134	02/01/2031	599.55	406.30	193.25	81,066.02
135	03/01/2031	599.55	405.33	194.22	80,871.80
136	04/01/2031	599.55	404.36	195.19	80,676.61
137	05/01/2031	599.55	403.38	196.17	80,480.44
138	06/01/2031	599.55	402.40	197.15	80,283.29
139	07/01/2031	599.55	401.42	198.13	80,085.16
140	08/01/2031	599.55	400.43	199.12	79,886.04
141	09/01/2031	599.55	399.43	200.12	79,685.92
142	10/01/2031	599.55	398.43	201.12	79,484.80
143	11/01/2031	599.55	397.42	202.13	79,282.67
144	12/01/2031	599.55	396.41	203.14	79,079.53
2031 TOTALS		**7,194.60**	**4,822.57**	**2,372.03**	
145	01/01/2032	599.55	395.40	204.15	78,875.38
146	02/01/2032	599.55	394.38	205.17	78,670.21
147	03/01/2032	599.55	393.35	206.20	78,464.01
148	04/01/2032	599.55	392.32	207.23	78,256.78
149	05/01/2032	599.55	391.28	208.27	78,048.51
150	06/01/2032	599.55	390.24	209.31	77,839.20
151	07/01/2032	599.55	389.20	210.35	77,628.85
152	08/01/2032	599.55	388.14	211.41	77,417.44
153	09/01/2032	599.55	387.09	212.46	77,204.98
154	10/01/2032	599.55	386.02	213.53	76,991.45
155	11/01/2032	599.55	384.96	214.59	76,776.86
156	12/01/2032	599.55	383.88	215.67	76,561.19

	DATE	PAYMENT	INTEREST	PRINCIPAL	BALANCE
2032 TOTALS		**7,194.60**	**4,676.26**	**2,518.34**	
157	01/01/2033	599.55	382.81	216.74	76,344.45
158	02/01/2033	599.55	381.72	217.83	76,126.62
159	03/01/2033	599.55	380.63	218.92	75,907.70
160	04/01/2033	599.55	379.54	220.01	75,687.69
161	05/01/2033	599.55	378.44	221.11	75,466.58
162	06/01/2033	599.55	377.33	222.22	75,244.36
163	07/01/2033	599.55	376.22	223.33	75,021.03
164	08/01/2033	599.55	375.11	224.44	74,796.59
165	09/01/2033	599.55	373.98	225.57	74,571.02
166	10/01/2033	599.55	372.86	226.69	74,344.33
167	11/01/2033	599.55	371.72	227.83	74,116.50
168	12/01/2033	599.55	370.58	228.97	73,887.53
2033 TOTALS		**7,194.60**	**4,520.94**	**2,673.66**	
169	01/01/2034	599.55	369.44	230.11	73,657.42
170	02/01/2034	599.55	368.29	231.26	73,426.16
171	03/01/2034	599.55	367.13	232.42	73,193.74
172	04/01/2034	599.55	365.97	233.58	72,960.16
173	05/01/2034	599.55	364.80	234.75	72,725.41
174	06/01/2034	599.55	363.63	235.92	72,489.49
175	07/01/2034	599.55	362.45	237.10	72,252.39
176	08/01/2034	599.55	361.26	238.29	72,014.10
177	09/01/2034	599.55	360.07	239.48	71,774.62
178	10/01/2034	599.55	358.87	240.68	71,533.94
179	11/01/2034	599.55	357.67	241.88	71,292.06
180	12/01/2034	599.55	356.46	243.09	71,048.97
2034 TOTALS		**7,194.60**	**4,356.04**	**2,838.56**	
181	01/01/2035	599.55	355.24	244.31	70,804.66
182	02/01/2035	599.55	354.02	245.53	70,559.13
183	03/01/2035	599.55	352.80	246.75	70,312.38
184	04/01/2035	599.55	351.56	247.99	70,064.39
185	05/01/2035	599.55	350.32	249.23	69,815.16
186	06/01/2035	599.55	349.08	250.47	69,564.69
187	07/01/2035	599.55	347.82	251.73	69,312.96
188	08/01/2035	599.55	346.56	252.99	69,059.97
189	09/01/2035	599.55	345.30	254.25	68,805.72
190	10/01/2035	599.55	344.03	255.52	68,550.20
191	11/01/2035	599.55	342.75	256.80	68,293.40
192	12/01/2035	599.55	341.47	258.08	68,035.32

	DATE	PAYMENT	INTEREST	PRINCIPAL	BALANCE
2035 TOTALS		**7,194.60**	**4,180.95**	**3,013.65**	
193	01/01/2036	599.55	340.18	259.37	67,775.95
194	02/01/2036	599.55	338.88	260.67	67,515.28
195	03/01/2036	599.55	337.58	261.97	67,253.31
196	04/01/2036	599.55	336.27	263.28	66,990.03
197	05/01/2036	599.55	334.95	264.60	66,725.43
198	06/01/2036	599.55	333.63	265.92	66,459.51
199	07/01/2036	599.55	332.30	267.25	66,192.26
200	08/01/2036	599.55	330.96	268.59	65,923.67
201	09/01/2036	599.55	329.62	269.93	65,653.74
202	10/01/2036	599.55	328.27	271.28	65,382.46
203	11/01/2036	599.55	326.91	272.64	65,109.82
204	12/01/2036	599.55	325.55	274.00	64,835.82
2036 TOTALS		**7,194.60**	**3,995.10**	**3,199.50**	
205	01/01/2037	599.55	324.18	275.37	64,560.45
206	02/01/2037	599.55	322.80	276.75	64,283.70
207	03/01/2037	599.55	321.42	278.13	64,005.57
208	04/01/2037	599.55	320.03	279.52	63,726.05
209	05/01/2037	599.55	318.63	280.92	63,445.13
210	06/01/2037	599.55	317.23	282.32	63,162.81
211	07/01/2037	599.55	315.81	283.74	62,879.07
212	08/01/2037	599.55	314.40	285.15	62,593.92
213	09/01/2037	599.55	312.97	286.58	62,307.34
214	10/01/2037	599.55	311.54	288.01	62,019.33
215	11/01/2037	599.55	310.10	289.45	61,729.88
216	12/01/2037	599.55	308.65	290.90	61,438.98
2037 TOTALS		**7,194.60**	**3,797.76**	**3,396.84**	
217	01/01/2038	599.55	307.19	292.36	61,146.62
218	02/01/2038	599.55	305.73	293.82	60,852.80
219	03/01/2038	599.55	304.26	295.29	60,557.51
220	04/01/2038	599.55	302.79	296.76	60,260.75
221	05/01/2038	599.55	301.30	298.25	59,962.50
222	06/01/2038	599.55	299.81	299.74	59,662.76
223	07/01/2038	599.55	298.31	301.24	59,361.52
224	08/01/2038	599.55	296.81	302.74	59,058.78
225	09/01/2038	599.55	295.29	304.26	58,754.52
226	10/01/2038	599.55	293.77	305.78	58,448.74
227	11/01/2038	599.55	292.24	307.31	58,141.43
228	12/01/2038	599.55	290.71	308.84	57,832.59

	DATE	PAYMENT	INTEREST	PRINCIPAL	BALANCE
2038 TOTALS		**7,194.60**	**3,588.21**	**3,606.39**	
229	01/01/2039	599.55	289.16	310.39	57,522.20
230	02/01/2039	599.55	287.61	311.94	57,210.26
231	03/01/2039	599.55	286.05	313.50	56,896.76
232	04/01/2039	599.55	284.48	315.07	56,581.69
233	05/01/2039	599.55	282.91	316.64	56,265.05
234	06/01/2039	599.55	281.33	318.22	55,946.83
235	07/01/2039	599.55	279.73	319.82	55,627.01
236	08/01/2039	599.55	278.14	321.41	55,305.60
237	09/01/2039	599.55	276.53	323.02	54,982.58
238	10/01/2039	599.55	274.91	324.64	54,657.94
239	11/01/2039	599.55	273.29	326.26	54,331.68
240	12/01/2039	599.55	271.66	327.89	54,003.79
2039 TOTALS		**7,194.60**	**3,365.80**	**3,828.80**	
241	01/01/2040	599.55	270.02	329.53	53,674.26
242	02/01/2040	599.55	268.37	331.18	53,343.08
243	03/01/2040	599.55	266.72	332.83	53,010.25
244	04/01/2040	599.55	265.05	334.50	52,675.75
245	05/01/2040	599.55	263.38	336.17	52,339.58
246	06/01/2040	599.55	261.70	337.85	52,001.73
247	07/01/2040	599.55	260.01	339.54	51,662.19
248	08/01/2040	599.55	258.31	341.24	51,320.95
249	09/01/2040	599.55	256.60	342.95	50,978.00
250	10/01/2040	599.55	254.89	344.66	50,633.34
251	11/01/2040	599.55	253.17	346.38	50,286.96
252	12/01/2040	599.55	251.43	348.12	49,938.84
2040 TOTALS		**7,194.60**	**3,129.65**	**4,064.95**	
253	01/01/2041	599.55	249.69	349.86	49,588.98
254	02/01/2041	599.55	247.94	351.61	49,237.37
255	03/01/2041	599.55	246.19	353.36	48,884.01
256	04/01/2041	599.55	244.42	355.13	48,528.88
257	05/01/2041	599.55	242.64	356.91	48,171.97
258	06/01/2041	599.55	240.86	358.69	47,813.28
259	07/01/2041	599.55	239.07	360.48	47,452.80
260	08/01/2041	599.55	237.26	362.29	47,090.51
261	09/01/2041	599.55	235.45	364.10	46,726.41
262	10/01/2041	599.55	233.63	365.92	46,360.49
263	11/01/2041	599.55	231.80	367.75	45,992.74
264	12/01/2041	599.55	229.96	369.59	45,623.15

	DATE	PAYMENT	INTEREST	PRINCIPAL	BALANCE
2041 TOTALS		**7,194.60**	**2,878.91**	**4,315.69**	
265	01/01/2042	599.55	228.12	371.43	45,251.72
266	02/01/2042	599.55	226.26	373.29	44,878.43
267	03/01/2042	599.55	224.39	375.16	44,503.27
268	04/01/2042	599.55	222.52	377.03	44,126.24
269	05/01/2042	599.55	220.63	378.92	43,747.32
270	06/01/2042	599.55	218.74	380.81	43,366.51
271	07/01/2042	599.55	216.83	382.72	42,983.79
272	08/01/2042	599.55	214.92	384.63	42,599.16
273	09/01/2042	599.55	213.00	386.55	42,212.61
274	10/01/2042	599.55	211.06	388.49	41,824.12
275	11/01/2042	599.55	209.12	390.43	41,433.69
276	12/01/2042	599.55	207.17	392.38	41,041.31
2042 TOTALS		**7,194.60**	**2,612.76**	**4,581.84**	
277	01/01/2043	599.55	205.21	394.34	40,646.97
278	02/01/2043	599.55	203.23	396.32	40,250.65
279	03/01/2043	599.55	201.25	398.30	39,852.35
280	04/01/2043	599.55	199.26	400.29	39,452.06
281	05/01/2043	599.55	197.26	402.29	39,049.77
282	06/01/2043	599.55	195.25	404.30	38,645.47
283	07/01/2043	599.55	193.23	406.32	38,239.15
284	08/01/2043	599.55	191.20	408.35	37,830.80
285	09/01/2043	599.55	189.15	410.40	37,420.40
286	10/01/2043	599.55	187.10	412.45	37,007.95
287	11/01/2043	599.55	185.04	414.51	36,593.44
288	12/01/2043	599.55	182.97	416.58	36,176.86
2043 TOTALS		**7,194.60**	**2,330.15**	**4,864.45**	
289	01/01/2044	599.55	180.88	418.67	35,758.19
290	02/01/2044	599.55	178.79	420.76	35,337.43
291	03/01/2044	599.55	176.69	422.86	34,914.57
292	04/01/2044	599.55	174.57	424.98	34,489.59
293	05/01/2044	599.55	172.45	427.10	34,062.49
294	06/01/2044	599.55	170.31	429.24	33,633.25
295	07/01/2044	599.55	168.17	431.38	33,201.87
296	08/01/2044	599.55	166.01	433.54	32,768.33
297	09/01/2044	599.55	163.84	435.71	32,332.62
298	10/01/2044	599.55	161.66	437.89	31,894.73
299	11/01/2044	599.55	159.47	440.08	31,454.65
300	12/01/2044	599.55	157.27	442.28	31,012.37

	DATE	PAYMENT	INTEREST	PRINCIPAL	BALANCE
2044 TOTALS		**7,194.60**	**2,030.11**	**5,164.49**	
301	01/01/2045	599.55	155.06	444.49	30,567.88
302	02/01/2045	599.55	152.84	446.71	30,121.17
303	03/01/2045	599.55	150.61	448.94	29,672.23
304	04/01/2045	599.55	148.36	451.19	29,221.04
305	05/01/2045	599.55	146.11	453.44	28,767.60
306	06/01/2045	599.55	143.84	455.71	28,311.89
307	07/01/2045	599.55	141.56	457.99	27,853.90
308	08/01/2045	599.55	139.27	460.28	27,393.62
309	09/01/2045	599.55	136.97	462.58	26,931.04
310	10/01/2045	599.55	134.66	464.89	26,466.15
311	11/01/2045	599.55	132.33	467.22	25,998.93
312	12/01/2045	599.55	129.99	469.56	25,529.37
2045 TOTALS		**7,194.60**	**1,711.60**	**5,483.00**	
313	01/01/2046	599.55	127.65	471.90	25,057.47
314	02/01/2046	599.55	125.29	474.26	24,583.21
315	03/01/2046	599.55	122.92	476.63	24,106.58
316	04/01/2046	599.55	120.53	479.02	23,627.56
317	05/01/2046	599.55	118.14	481.41	23,146.15
318	06/01/2046	599.55	115.73	483.82	22,662.33
319	07/01/2046	599.55	113.31	486.24	22,176.09
320	08/01/2046	599.55	110.88	488.67	21,687.42
321	09/01/2046	599.55	108.44	491.11	21,196.31
322	10/01/2046	599.55	105.98	493.57	20,702.74
323	11/01/2046	599.55	103.51	496.04	20,206.70
324	12/01/2046	599.55	101.03	498.52	19,708.18
2046 TOTALS		**7,194.60**	**1,373.41**	**5,821.19**	
325	01/01/2047	599.55	98.54	501.01	19,207.17
326	02/01/2047	599.55	96.04	503.51	18,703.66
327	03/01/2047	599.55	93.52	506.03	18,197.63
328	04/01/2047	599.55	90.99	508.56	17,689.07
329	05/01/2047	599.55	88.45	511.10	17,177.97
330	06/01/2047	599.55	85.89	513.66	16,664.31
331	07/01/2047	599.55	83.32	516.23	16,148.08
332	08/01/2047	599.55	80.74	518.81	15,629.27
333	09/01/2047	599.55	78.15	521.40	15,107.87
334	10/01/2047	599.55	75.54	524.01	14,583.86
335	11/01/2047	599.55	72.92	526.63	14,057.23
336	12/01/2047	599.55	70.29	529.26	13,527.97

	DATE	PAYMENT	INTEREST	PRINCIPAL	BALANCE
2047 TOTALS		**7,194.60**	**1,014.39**	**6,180.21**	
337	01/01/2048	599.55	67.64	531.91	12,996.06
338	02/01/2048	599.55	64.98	534.57	12,461.49
339	03/01/2048	599.55	62.31	537.24	11,924.25
340	04/01/2048	599.55	59.62	539.93	11,384.32
341	05/01/2048	599.55	56.92	542.63	10,841.69
342	06/01/2048	599.55	54.21	545.34	10,296.35
343	07/01/2048	599.55	51.48	548.07	9,748.28
344	08/01/2048	599.55	48.74	550.81	9,197.47
345	09/01/2048	599.55	45.99	553.56	8,643.91
346	10/01/2048	599.55	43.22	556.33	8,087.58
347	11/01/2048	599.55	40.44	559.11	7,528.47
348	12/01/2048	599.55	37.64	561.91	6,966.56
2048 TOTALS		**7,194.60**	**633.19**	**6,561.41**	
349	01/01/2049	599.55	34.83	564.72	6,401.84
350	02/01/2049	599.55	32.01	567.54	5,834.30
351	03/01/2049	599.55	29.17	570.38	5,263.92
352	04/01/2049	599.55	26.32	573.23	4,690.69
353	05/01/2049	599.55	23.45	576.10	4,114.59
354	06/01/2049	599.55	20.57	578.98	3,535.61
355	07/01/2049	599.55	17.68	581.87	2,953.74
356	08/01/2049	599.55	14.77	584.78	2,368.96
357	09/01/2049	599.55	11.84	587.71	1,781.25
358	10/01/2049	599.55	8.91	590.64	1,190.61
359	11/01/2049	599.55	5.95	593.60	597.01
360	12/01/2049	599.55	2.54	597.01	0.00
2049 TOTALS			**7,194.60**	**228.04**	**6,966.56**
GRAND TOTALS		**215,838.00**	**115,838.00**	**100,000.00**	**12,996.06**

FIGURE 2.1. AMORTIZATION TABLE FOR A $100,000 LOAN WITH 30 YEAR TERM AND 6% INTEREST RATE

DISCOUNT

Notes are typically bought and sold at a discount to the amount owed, and the discount does not impact the amount owed in any way. For example, if a note with a balance of $100,000 is sold at a discount to an investor for $81,710.13, the investor has purchased the right to collect the entire amount due on the note. When the loan is paid off (due to the property being sold or refinanced), the current loan balance less any amortized principal payments will be the amount due. This allows for a potential profit of $15,000 in this example, and when a payoff happens unexpectedly, it can drive up the rate of return significantly. The average life span of a mortgage in the US has historically been five to seven years before a property is sold or refinanced, so if you are holding a note for the long term, you will likely encounter this scenario.

Continuing with our example, let's take a closer look at this transaction. This note has a balance due of $100,000, thirty-year term, 6% interest rate, and a monthly principal-and-interest payment (P&I) of $599.55. The note is purchased at a discount for $81,710.13, which will then provide a yield of 8% to the investor that bought the note.

We can calculate the annual return on investment by dividing the annual income (one year of payments) by the cost of the note.

Note Principal Balance = $100,000.00

Purchase Price = $81,710.13

Monthly P&I payment = $599.55

Yearly income = 12 months × $599.55 = $7,194.72

Return on investment (ROI) = Annual Income / Purchase Price

ROI = $7,194.72 / $81,710.13 = 0.8805 = 8.8%

Let's say that three full years go by, and then the borrower sells the property. Just before the property settlement, the title company contacts the loan servicer to request a payoff. The loan servicer calculates the payoff using the $100,000 original loan amount and the thirty-year amortization table to determine how much principal has been paid over the three-year time frame and confirms the payoff amount at $95,964.94. At settlement, the loan is then paid off, and a check for $95,964.94 is paid out to the lender from the proceeds of the sale. Note the difference between the payoff amount and the purchase price of the note.

Now we can look at the total rate of return for this investment, when we annualize it over the three years that the note was held.

Total amount invested: $81,710.13

Amount received from loan payoff: $95,964.94

Amount received in monthly payments:
$599.55 × 36 months = $21,584.16

Total amount received =
$95,964.94 + $21,584.16 = $117,549.10

Total gain (profit) = $35,838.97

Annualized return (ROI) = 12.89%

The interesting detail about loan payoffs is that they are likely to happen, keeping in mind the national statistic that the average life span of a mortgage in the US is between five and seven years. Additionally, they are completely random, and are something that the lender has no control over. It is important to remember that homeowners are people that have busy lives with ever-changing circumstances. You just never know when a person suddenly may need to sell a property because they have to move for job relocation or their family size has increased or decreased, or because it makes financial sense to refinance their mortgage. This randomness makes for an exciting and dynamic part of being in the note business!

In a note, there are four parameters: loan amount, payment amount, interest rate, and term (typically expressed in months). If we know three variables, we can always solve for the fourth, using a financial calculator. The most well-known financial calculator is the Hewlett Packard HP12C; however, today there are many financial calculators available as online applications or smartphone applications that run on your mobile device. For a deep dive into using financial calculators specifically for note investing, I highly recommend reading the book *Invest in Debt* by Jimmy Napier.

FIGURE 2.2. PHOTO OF THE CLASSIC HEWLETT PACKARD HP12C FINANCIAL CALCULATOR.

KEY CONCEPTS

- A primary objective of note investing is the acquisition of a payment stream or cash flow at a discount relative to the amount of the debt.
- There is a distinct difference between a note and a mortgage. The note is a promissory note or contract, a "promise to pay." The mortgage (or deed of trust) is a security interest, which provides for the borrower to give collateral to the lender in order to secure the note. The action of recording the mortgage document in the public record at the county courthouse is known as "perfecting the lien."
- Some of the ways to get involved in note investing: originating a note through seller financing when selling a property, purchasing an existing note directly from a seller, or investing in a note fund.
- As illustrated in the example in this chapter, it is possible to earn a superior rate of return through investing in notes. One can see how including this type of investment as part of an overall investment portfolio could significantly make up for any below-average returns in other investments.

3

THE NOTE BUSINESS

WHY NOTES ARE SOLD AT A DISCOUNT!

Compound interest is the eighth wonder of the world.
He who understands it, earns it; he who doesn't, pays it.

—Albert Einstein, physicist and Nobel Prize winner

In this chapter, we will discuss the note business at a high level, and we will take a look at the secondary market that exists for the buying and selling of debt. Did you know that all kinds of debt are bundled and packaged, and then bought and sold every day on the secondary market? These are typically very large transactions between financial institutions in which mortgages are bundled into pools of hundreds or even thousands of loans for the purpose of commercial transactions.

If you have ever taken out a mortgage when purchasing or refinancing a property, you may have noticed that typically three to six months after closing on the loan, you receive a friendly letter in the mail notifying you that the bank or lender has sold the loan and that, as of the upcoming transfer date, you should send your payments to the new lender moving forward. Also, this notice tells you that the terms and conditions that were agreed to in the loan documents are not changing in any way.

Federal banking laws in the United States allow banks and financial institutions to sell mortgages, and consumer/borrower consent is not required when this takes place. The financial institution is required to disclose the transaction and to send by mail the required notices to the borrower. If you are curious, you can check on the websites of Fannie Mae or Freddie Mac. (These are the quasi-governmental institutions involved in the majority of mortgage loans in the United States.) There, you will see detailed information about current and prior loan sales, including information about the number of loans, the average loan size, and the total amount of the transactions.

Why do lenders sell mortgages? If we take a moment to think about banks and lending institutions, their business model is to originate new loans—lots of loans, over and over. This is the essence of the concept of the velocity of money, which is to continuously turn over and redeploy that capital. Keeping that in mind, the lender will originate the loan, sell it off in order to recoup its capital, then will use that capital to originate a new loan, continuing on in that cycle. Lenders do need to keep a large amount of capital liquid and available so that they can continue lending and originating new loans.

Another reason why banks and lending institutions sell their loans is that they make a profit during the loan origination and the sale, and they can afford to sell the loans to the buyer at a slight discount from what is owed. Banks make money by charging points and origination fees with the processing and setup of a new loan and by collecting interest from the monthly payments. Keep in mind that during the first years of a loan amortization schedule, most of the monthly payment goes to interest, and very little goes to the loan principal.

Understand that notes and mortgages are sold and traded on the secondary market every day. At the top level, we have the large banking institutions as well as lending entities, such as Fannie Mae and Freddie Mac. These institutions sell loans to larger hedge funds and to private equity firms. The loans are then sold to smaller funds and to individual investors.

CASE STUDY: HOUSTON, TEXAS

This note was purchased as a performing note that had been modified by the previous note owner into a fifteen-year (180-month) term. In return for the substantial discount that was being offered, we were willing to take on the additional risk of a short payment history. In this case, the payment history was two months. This note was purchased in a self-directed IRA account, and there was little activity involved beyond monitoring the servicing transfer, as the two servicing companies involved went through the process to transition the payment stream from the note seller to our IRA account. An interesting detail on this note is that after receiving about six years of payments, we would have received back all our initial capital investment that was used to purchase the note.

NOTE DETAILS

Monthly Payment Amount = $371.95

Remaining payments = 178

Interest rate = 9%

Principal balance = $36,671

Lien position = second position

TRANSACTION DETAILS

Note Purchase price = $26,500

Annual cash flow = $4,463.40

Rate of return = 15% per year

KEY CONCEPTS

- There exists an entire secondary mortgage market where loans are bought and sold every day.
- The business model for banks and mortgage loan originators is to originate loans at a high volume, with a high velocity of money. They will originate loans and then, almost immediately, sell the loans in order to recoup their capital and then go back out to originate new loans to their ...mers. This is the main reason why many lenders will ... their mortgages soon after loan origination.

4

EVALUATING A NOTE

THE RELATIONSHIP BETWEEN RISK AND YIELD

Successful investing is about managing risk, not avoiding it.

—Benjamin Graham, investor and economist

Notes are bought and sold with pricing based on many variables. For an investor looking to purchase a note, the first parameter that must be considered is the desired yield. Notes can be bought with a wide range of yields, keeping in mind the concept that there is a direct relationship between yield and risk. The lower the yield, the lower the risk and the safer the note. Notes that are super safe, backed by excellent collateral, and well protected with a large equity position might pay a return in the range of 4% to 8%. However, if you have an appetite for higher-yielding investments and are willing to take on more risk, you will be able to find notes out there that pay a return of 18% or more, with the trade-off that these might have less desirable collateral or lower amounts of equity. Which type of note is best for you? It is important to consider that this is a very personal decision based on your own experience and risk tolerance, and there is no right or wrong answer. Perhaps an investor just starting out may decide that they want to acquire some notes of each type in an effort to build a well-rounded note portfolio.

The next concept to be discussed revolves around the discount at which a note is sold and how that impacts the note buyer's rate of return. Let's take the example of a thirty-year note, which was illustrated in Figure 2.1, with a principal balance (often referred to as the Unpaid Principal Balance, or UPB) of $100,000, an interest rate of 6%, and a monthly payment amount of $599.55.

The holder of the note may find themselves in a situation in which they wish to quickly raise capital to put toward another project or another investment opportunity, and they are willing to sell their note at a discount. When this note is sold, keep in mind that from the perspective of the borrower, all the terms and conditions agreed to in the note will remain the same. There is no change of any kind in the interest rate, term, and payment amount. The table in Figure 4.1 illustrates how different discounts he purchase price of this note will impact the rate of return yer of the note.

DISCOUNTED PURCHASE PRICE	RATE OF RETURN
$90,118.41	7%
$81,710.13	8%
$74,514.44	9%
$68,320.35	10%

FIGURE 4.1. ILLUSTRATION OF HOW THE DISCOUNTED PURCHASE PRICE IMPACTS THE RATE OF RETURN

When you are negotiating to purchase a note from a note seller, the main considerations to keep in mind are your risk tolerance and the rate of return you are willing to accept for your capital. Based on that rate of return, you can use a financial calculator or spreadsheet software to determine a valuation for the note at your desired rate of return (this is called a "present value," or PV, in the financial calculator), and that becomes your discounted offer price.

You may find yourself asking which types of notes to buy. A significant driver for your note purchase decisions will revolve around your risk tolerance. Note investing is full of risks, many of which can be managed effectively with good systems and good counsel. A newer investor who is just starting out in the business will naturally have a lower risk tolerance for the type of notes they will buy. Over time, as the investor becomes more experienced and as they develop their skills in becoming a better problem solver, the risk tolerance will change and evolve. As with most investments, notes that are lower in risk will be more expensive to acquire and, therefore, will yield a lower return. Conversely, the notes that are higher risk and have more problems needing to be solved will be less expensive to acquire and will yield a higher return.

Let's take a brief look at some of the risk/reward parameters that may be encountered with note investing, each one being listed on a spectrum in order from lowest risk to highest risk. In the next chapter, Performing Due Diligence, we discuss many of these in further detail so that they can be evaluated and considered prior to purchase and then be dealt with accordingly.

EQUITY COVERAGE:

- Full equity, where the market value of the property is greater than or equal to the amount owed on the note (lowest risk)
- Partial equity, where the market value of the property is enough to only partially cover the amount owed on the note
- No equity or negative equity, where the market value of the property is not enough to cover the amount owed for taxes or other senior liens (highest risk)

LIEN POSITION:

- Senior position or first position; typically there are no senior liens other than property taxes (lowest risk)
- Junior liens or second mortgages; often originated as home equity loans or home equity lines of credit (HELOCs)
- Unsecured liens, where the note is not secured by any property (highest risk)

PAYMENT HISTORY:

- Current for prior twelve months (lowest risk)
- Current but with one or more late payments within previous twelve months
- Rolling thirty days late (monthly payments are being made consistently, thirty days late)
- Rolling sixty to ninety days late (monthly payments are being made consistently, sixty to ninety days late)
- A note in default, no payments made for the past ninety days (highest risk)

(Note: Rolling late is when payments are thirty or sixty days behind; however, a monthly payment is being made each month consistently in an effort to get fully caught back up.)

TITLE-RELATED ISSUES:

- Mortgage is properly recorded with clean chain of assignments (lowest risk)
- Missing or broken chain of assignment
- Title issues requiring a claim to title insurance
- Title/lien issues requiring a "quiet title" action in court, costing significant time and expense to resolve (highest risk)

(Note: An assignment of mortgage is a legal document that is associated with a particular mortgage. In the same way that a deed transfers ownership of property from the seller to the buyer, the assignment of mortgage transfers the ownership of a mortgage from seller to buyer and is recorded in the county where the property is located.)

TAXES AND HOA FEES:

- Taxes and HOA (homeowners association) fees are current (lowest risk)
- Taxes and/or HOA fees are delinquent and will require reinstatement by the lender in order to protect their lien position (highest risk)

GEOGRAPHY AND LOCAL REAL ESTATE MARKET:

- Property located in a desirable or growing market with increasing property values (lowest risk)
- Property located in an undesirable or declining market with decreasing property values (highest risk)

STATE-SPECIFIC FORECLOSURE TIMELINES:

- Nonjudicial states with shorter foreclosure timelines of three to six months (lowest risk)
- Judicial states with longer foreclosure timelines of twelve to thirty-six months (highest risk)

(Note: In a judicial foreclosure state, the lender or noteholder has to file a lawsuit in court in order to foreclose. In a nonjudicial foreclosure state, the lender or noteholder can foreclose without going to court by instead using a trustee to handle the foreclosure, resulting in a faster timeline.)

BORROWER HISTORY:

- A clean financial history with good credit (lowest risk)
- Poor financial history with blemished credit
- Prior bankruptcies and/or judgments
- Current active bankruptcies (highest risk)

As detailed above, there are numerous factors that can be used to evaluate and assess risk. With risks in investing, those that are willing to take more risk can often be handsomely rewarded. There are no right or wrong answers, and this is something that each investor must carefully consider before getting started. For newer investors, it is sometimes better to accept a lower rate of return with less risk while they get started and learn the business. Over time, as their level of experience and expertise increases, investors will generally become more comfortable with taking on greater levels of risk and seeking higher returns.

CASE STUDY: RIVERSIDE, CALIFORNIA

This note was purchased as a performing note that had been modified by the previous note owner into a thirty-year (360-month) term. In return for the substantial discount that was being offered, we were willing to take on the additional risk of a short payment history. In this case, the payment history was eight months. Another benefit to us was that the note was already being serviced at the same servicer that we were using; therefore, the transfer of the note was expected to be very smooth and straightforward. This note was purchased in a self-directed IRA account, and there was little activity involved beyond monitoring the servicer as they transitioned the payment stream from the note seller to our IRA account.

NOTE DETAILS

Monthly payment amount = $358.06

Remaining payments = 352 months

Interest rate = 4%

Principal balance = $74,359.99

Lien position = second position

TRANSACTION DETAILS

Note purchase price = $27,200

Annual cash flow = $4,296.72

Rate of return = 15.6% per year

KEY CONCEPTS

- When purchasing a loan, the discount from the amount owed is what will drive up the investor's rate of return.
- Notes that have increased risk characteristics will be priced in the marketplace to generate a higher rate of return, and conversely, notes with lower risk characteristics will generate a lower rate of return.
- Consider your level of risk tolerance and experience before purchasing loans. Newer investors who are getting started in note investing will typically have better results (and a better investor experience) by starting out investing in lower-risk loans.

5

PERFORMING DUE DILIGENCE

Risk comes from not knowing what you're doing.

—Warren Buffett, investor and philanthropist

Note investing is very much a "buyer beware" activity, and the buyer alone is responsible for assessing the quality of a note before purchase. This is something that cannot be stressed enough, and it is extremely important that note investors develop this skill and their due diligence processes thoroughly in order to properly evaluate and manage risk. It is possible to lose a large amount of money very quickly if not performed correctly and with a strict attention to detail. Think of due diligence as the process of performing detective or forensic work, in which you check and verify every detail of the transaction. Never ever take the information provided to you by a note seller without reconfirming everything yourself as thoroughly as possible. Oftentimes, the information might be thirty days old and quickly becomes out of date, or something has changed just yesterday, or there was a critical data point that was unintentionally (or even intentionally) omitted. You will often uncover surprises that, if discovered prior to the transaction, can be used as a negotiation point for determining the price and terms of the purchase of the asset. Yes, you will undoubtedly make some mistakes or miss something along the way. Simply use it as a learning opportunity to improve your process and strive never to make the same mistake more than once. The repetition, refinement, and constant development of your due diligence process will make you a better and more skilled note investor in the long run.

In this chapter, we will cover the various aspects of performing due diligence in preparation for the purchase of a performing note. Due diligence may be broken down into the following four categories, and we will look at each of them in detail: the loan collateral file and loan documents, the borrower, the property, and the note seller.

LOAN COLLATERAL FILE AND LOAN DOCUMENTS

The loan collateral file typically will be made available in electronic form for your review and should consist of, at a minimum, the note, mortgage or deed of trust, assignments of mortgage, allonges (an allonge is an endorsement of the note to a new owner; the concept is similar to how a check can be endorsed over to a new payee), and loan modification or workout agreement (if the loan was ever modified).

If the loan was institutionally originated, meaning that it was originated by a bank or traditional lender, then it is likely that the loan documents were created using standardized and state-specific Fannie Mae and Freddie Mac document forms, and you should be able to review these on your own once you get comfortable with the documents. If the loan was originated as part of an owner-financed transaction or a commercial loan, it is recommended that you engage your attorney (preferably licensed to practice law in the state where the property is located) to provide support with your document review. Paying for one or two hours of your attorney's time to guide you through this process will be money well spent in this case, particularly if you are new to note investing. You can use it as a learning opportunity to better understand the important questions to be considered during due diligence, even if you do not end up buying the note that you are analyzing! Remember that you will pay for your education either up front before you buy or later on from living with the mistakes that were made. Paying up front always costs less and is the preferred method!

Keep in mind that the note will contain the details of the loan, such as the names of the borrowers, amount borrowed, interest rate, payment amount, and payment term. You will want to review these carefully and compare against what was originally being offered by the note seller. If there are any deviations of the interest rate, payment amount, or payment term, then it is possible that the note was modified under a loan modification or a workout agreement, and you will also want to review these documents, if applicable. This is your opportunity to ask all the questions before you commit contractually to the purchase transaction by signing a purchase and sale agreement, so it is best to ask up front.

MORTGAGE OR DEED OF TRUST

The mortgage or deed of trust is the security instrument that grants a lien or encumbrance against the property in favor of the lender. Reviewing this document, you will see references to the mortgagor (the property owner) and the mortgagee (the lender). The mortgagor is the borrower who is taking a loan and is pledging their property as security for repayment of this loan. The mortgagee is the lender who is giving the loan to the mortgagor and is receiving a security interest in the property from the property owner. This mortgage document is typically signed and notarized, and then will be recorded in the county courthouse or county recorder of the county in which the property is located, effectively "perfecting" the lien. Perfecting a lien refers to the legal process that establishes a lender's priority against other creditors or lien holders, and that gives the lender the right to foreclose in the event of a default. The act of recording the mortgage also puts the general public on notice that there is now a lien recorded against the property.

ASSIGNMENT OF MORTGAGE (OR ASSIGNMENT OF DEED OF TRUST)

The assignment is a document that officially confirms the transfer of a mortgage from one lender to another. When a note is sold, part of the sale will involve the lender selling the note to issue an assignment of mortgage to the buyer of the note. This assignment is a simple one-page document that details the subject property, the deed reference information, the original mortgage amount, the assignor (the lender selling the note), and the assignee (the investor buying the note). This assignment is then recorded in the public record and communicates that the mortgage was sold or transferred to a new owner, who will handle resolving the lien or releasing the lien when the loan has been satisfied or paid off. In many cases a mortgage will be transacted and sold multiple times over the life of the mortgage, resulting in a series of these assignment of mortgage documents having been recorded in the public record. This is known as the chain of assignment, and this will detail the chain of ownership of a mortgage from the current lender all the way back to the originating lender. A title report run against the property should pick up the mortgage and all the subsequent assignments of mortgage.

ALLONGE

The allonge is an endorsement to the note, where the lender is giving the right to collect on the note over to the new owner of the note. The allonge can be stamped as an endorsement on the back of one of the pages of the note, or it can be a separate document that is attached and then becomes part of the note. Similar to how a check can be endorsed by the receiver over to a third party, the allonge is what transfers all collection rights that are represented in the note over to another individual.

Just as the mortgage and the note are two separate and distinct functional documents, the assignment is the document that transfers the rights of the mortgage, and the allonge is the document that transfers the rights of the note.

LOAN MODIFICATION OR WORKOUT AGREEMENT

If the loan was previously in default and then was modified or renegotiated in order to be brought back to a current status, then there will be documentation in the loan file to reflect this agreement. The loan modification or workout agreement is documented using a mutual agreement between the lender and the borrower to waive any existing defaults and to restructure the terms of the loan. This agreement details the financial terms of the reinstatement, documenting any missed payments, any payments being made toward arrears, any amounts being deferred to the end of the loan term, and other conditions that were mutually agreed upon.

In addition to the loan documents, you will be reviewing loan details and information that is being provided by the loan seller. Most often, this will be provided in the form of a spreadsheet (also known as a "tape") and will contain, at minimum, the following pertinent details about the loan:

- Loan number
- UPB (this is the current Unpaid Principal Balance)
- Original UPB (at the time of loan origination)
- Property value
- Senior lien status (if you are evaluating a junior lien)
- Next payment due date (on a performing note on which payments are current, this date will be a date out in the future)
- Payment amount
- Payment term and how many payments remain
- Interest rate

Now, with the above information and with the help of your financial calculator (or an amortization table that you have constructed for this loan), you will want to use the current UPB to reference where in the payment schedule the loan currently is and cross-reference the number of remaining payments. If you find any large discrepancies, this will point to the possibility of a balloon payment due at the note maturity (if this is the case, you will see the balloon payment reflected in the note document) or a loan modification that was implemented with the borrower (if this is the case, you will want to make sure that you receive a copy of the signed agreement for your review).

DON'T LET SMALL DETAILS STAND IN THE WAY OF BIG PROGRESS.

William, a fellow note investor, was recently telling me about a rather alarming problem he encountered on a note he had purchased. During his review of the loan file, he was utterly shocked to find that the mortgage and all subsequent mortgage assignment documents were recorded in a county that was not where the subject property was actually located! The loan had been originated several years prior, and strangely enough no one had ever picked up on the error. This meant that the note he purchased was basically an unsecured note, resulting in a major risk to him as the note owner and a significantly lower value for that note. If the borrower were to refinance or sell the property, the mortgage would likely not have been paid off and the note would have remained as an unsecured loan. Since this was a problem that was discovered after he already owned the note, it was William's full responsibility to correct the problem and take on the costs involved in the resolution. Sometimes there are cities or towns that actually span across multiple counties or multiple municipalities, and this can result in mistakes being made during the origination and recording of a mortgage loan (for example, consider the confusion that could arise between the city of Charleston in South Carolina, and the city of Charleston in West Virginia). However, all hope was not lost in this case. Through working with a competent local real estate attorney, this problem was corrected and resolved. This resolution ended up taking about nine months of time along with the expense of legal costs. Once the resolution was complete, the loan was then fully secured by the property, and the result was that the note returned to realizing its full market value. Not long after this happened, William happened to be telling this story to a friend about how the little details tend to scare many people away, but by having a competent attorney on your team to help navigate the waters, these types of problems can be readily solved. The lesson is to not let the little details stand in the way of big progress.

THE BORROWER

The borrower information is typically provided in the loan spreadsheet or tape. This consists of the personal information of the borrower and coborrower: name, address, social security number, and so on. Some note sellers will be able to provide a recent credit report on the borrower. Any reputable note seller will require you to have signed an NDA (nondisclosure agreement) prior to sharing any borrower's personal financial information with you for evaluation purposes. Understand that it is perfectly legal for you, as a potential note buyer, to have access to this information. However, with that access also comes tremendous responsibility. You absolutely must handle the information in a responsible, secure, and ethical manner.

Some loan files will also include the original loan application at the time of origination; however, after months and years have elapsed since origination, the value of this information becomes less important to you.

Of greater importance is the current servicer's loan payment history, which will provide you with a good look at the track record of the loan and the borrower payments. The longer the payment history, the lower the risk of a default on the loan.

THE PROPERTY

In the evaluation of the property, you will want to ascertain the quality of the property that is the security for the loan. In today's modern age of technology and innovation, evaluating the property from afar is easier than ever, and this allows us to buy notes nationwide on properties that we have never seen (and that we may never see) in person. When you are performing your initial due diligence, you can utilize a combination of free and/or paid methods, outlined below, that are available to you so that you can arrive at a general valuation range for the property. As a part of this process, you will be determining how much equity is covering the payoff amount for the loan. A higher amount of equity coverage equates to lower risk and a higher price to be paid for the note. Conversely, a lower amount of equity coverage equates to higher risk and a lower price to be paid for the note. Notes are bought and sold all the time with full equity coverage, partial equity coverage, no equity coverage, or even negative equity coverage. Referring back to the previous section on note price and yield, this will directly impact your rate of return.

ELEMENTS OF DUE DILIGENCE

- **Internet mapping websites and tools.** Online search engines that quickly display satellite photos and street view photos for the property. Be sure to try multiple search engines and pay attention to the date stamp in the image; it might be from several years ago. Zoom all the way in and take a look at the property and the adjacent houses; this will give you a feel for the neighborhood. You can get a general sense of the condition of the property based on the exterior of the house and how the grounds are maintained. You will know the difference right away between seeing a well-maintained property exterior and landscaping or a blue tarp on the roof along with several junk cars in the driveway and a lawn that is sixteen inches high. You will also want to note if the property is located in an urban, suburban, or rural area.

- **Property valuation websites.** Online property valuation websites that utilize proprietary algorithms based on comparable sales in the area.
- **Real estate sales websites.** Multiple listing websites that will show past history on the property if it was previously listed for sale (sometimes with interior photos), as well as other active sales in the area.
- **Local real estate agents and brokers.** Picking up the telephone and calling a local real estate agent who handles sales in that town or neighborhood. If you observe in your research that there is a real estate agent with several active listings in the neighborhood, that is an excellent place to start. Real estate agents are usually happy to speak with you and are a good source of information on the area and on the local real estate market. Be up front that you are doing research about the local market, that you are looking to establish a relationship with a real estate agent in the area, and be respectful of their time.
- **Field visit/exterior inspection.** There are numerous property inspection vendors who utilize a nationwide network of agents who can provide this service for a low cost. This will be money well spent, and absolutely nothing beats having local boots on the ground to have a look on your behalf.
- **Verification of lien position.** If you are purchasing a first position mortgage, you will certainly want to verify that your mortgage is actually in first position. This can be done through an inexpensive title report called an owner and encumbrance report (often called an O&E report). These are available through any title report vendor for a low cost and will get turned around typically within twenty-four

hours. It is not generally necessary to run a full title search, which will be much more expensive and will take several days to complete. If you are not familiar with looking at and interpreting the O&E report, do not hesitate to request additional support in reviewing the results of the report from the title report vendor or from your attorney.

- **HOA liens.** If the property is located in a community with a condo association or a homeowners association (HOA), you will want to utilize the O&E report to check for any HOA liens or HOA dues that are outstanding.
- **Status of senior liens.** If you are evaluating a junior lien, you will want to review the credit report to confirm the current status of the senior lien.
- **Taxes and municipal liens.** This is an often overlooked detail. Take this as a very serious risk and do not rely on county websites or online records. Again, picking up the telephone and speaking with a live person in the local property tax collector's office can uncover valuable information. Check the status of taxes to see if they are current. Sometimes you might find that taxes have not been paid in several years and that the property is scheduled for a tax sale! In many states, when the property is sold at a tax sale, the liens and mortgages will get wiped out (extinguished). As you can see, it is a very good thing that you discovered this before you purchased the note, right?

THE NOTE SELLER

There is a fair amount of due diligence that you will need to perform on the note seller or the principals of the company you are dealing with. Do you know them and have any kind of preexisting relationship with them? Or is it someone that you just randomly met online a week ago? Will you run a background check on the note seller to see if any prior civil or criminal activity turns up?

Keep in mind that when you buy a note, you will be signing a contract and then sending a wire transfer to purchase the note. Think about your recourse if you were to find yourself in the unfortunate position of having wired your purchase funding and then not ever receiving your loan file. If you are not dealing with a reputable person or entity, you may encounter many challenges postclosing, such as:

- Receiving your loan collateral file, complete with all documents
- Supporting the servicing transfer from the seller's servicer to the buyer's servicer
- Delivering a note that matches the characteristics that were represented to you prior to the sale

In dealing with a reputable note seller, they will be responsive and supportive to any of the above issues if they arise. I will point out that problems certainly do arise. Having a good relationship with your note seller, with open communication, will facilitate a prompt resolution of any issues or problems that come up during or after the transaction.

The note industry is a very small, very tight-knit community, and mostly everyone knows each other, directly or indirectly. Word travels very fast about a note seller that received a purchase wire transfer and did not deliver as agreed, as well as a note buyer that signed a purchase agreement and then did not close on their transaction. Reputation is everything in this business, and it is of utmost importance that you conduct all business transactions in the most legal and ethical manner possible. Between your relationships with other note investors, vendors, and attorneys that are active in the business, it should not be difficult to find out who has done business in the past with your note seller. The note seller will likely be doing the same to qualify you as the buyer. You may even go as far as to ask for references if this is an unfamiliar individual that you are dealing with for the first time. Consider it a serious red flag if a note seller is not able to immediately tell you where the physical loan collateral is located (it could be stored in their own local office or stored off-site at a document custodian) and who is currently servicing the loan.

Remember that you will be spending a significant investment of your time and some money in conducting your due diligence. If you find a fatal flaw or an issue that is unacceptable to you, it is better to blow up the deal early on in the due diligence process rather than waste people's time, including your own. It is best practice to clearly state the reasons why you have decided to decline to the seller, and then decide whether to try to renegotiate your purchase price, or simply pass on the transaction and move on.

KEY CONCEPTS

- The skill of performing due diligence is one of the most important skills that a note investor will need in order to be successful. Spend time developing these skills, and seek to continuously refine and improve them as your experience level grows.
- When evaluating a note, the due diligence can be broken down into four primary categories: the loan documents, the borrower, the property, and the note seller.

6

THE LOAN PURCHASE TRANSACTION

The rich invest their money and spend what is left;
the poor spend their money and invest what is left.

—Jim Rohn, author and motivational speaker

The transaction for a loan purchase is fairly straightforward. Once the buyer has completed their due diligence and has reached agreement on a price with the seller, they will sign a note purchase agreement. This agreement covers the details of the transaction and any terms and conditions that will be part of the sale. There will be responsibilities for both the buyer and seller with time frames, as well as a detailed schedule of the notes that are being sold. This is a binding contract; therefore, be sure that you understand all the terms, and, of course, it is recommended to engage your attorney as needed to provide legal support during the review process.

I will call attention to one section of the agreement called "Representations and Warrants." The scope of the representations that are being made can vary widely. Some will have a very limited scope, simply stating that the seller is a valid and legitimate entity, and that they have full and complete rights to sell the note. On the other end of the spectrum, you may see representations about the validity and enforceability of the lien, the lien position, loan balances, and other characteristics. There is nothing standard, and these points are all negotiable between buyer and seller.

Once the agreement has been signed by both parties, then funding the purchase should happen via a wire transfer to the seller's bank account, followed by delivery of the loan collateral file (the original loan documents), and then the servicing transfer from the seller's note servicer to the buyer's note servicer. There is a window of time defined for the buyer to be able to go back to the seller for recourse in case of any missing loan documents or other issues with the physical loan file. The servicing transfer is typically set to be thirty to sixty days or more out into the future to allow for compliance notices and disclosures to be sent out by the servicers. The dates for each of these activities should be clearly spelled out in the note sale agreement.

There are some attorneys that will act in the capacity of an escrow agent, where they (for a fee) will handle the transaction much like a title agent or closing agent handles the conveyance of a property, receiving the funds into escrow and then releasing the loan collateral file to the buyer once everything is complete. If you decide to go this route, you as the buyer will be expected to handle all costs involved to compensate the attorney for providing this service. The use of an escrow or closing agent is more common on larger trades where many notes are being sold as part of a single transaction.

KEY CONCEPTS

- The note purchase agreement is a binding legal contract that you will be signing as the note buyer. It is highly recommended that you retain legal counsel to support you with a review of the contract and to provide a detailed explanation of any clauses or terms that you do not fully understand.
- Pay special attention to the section of the agreement that details the representations and warrants.
- Adhere strictly to all time frames for closing and funding the transaction. Your performance as a buyer will define your reputation moving forward in the note industry.

7

BOARDING THE LOAN

When life gives you lemons, make lemonade and sell it for a profit!

—Author Unknown

Following the completion of the loan purchase transaction, in which the consideration for the purchase has been sent by bank wire to the loan seller, and the note seller has delivered the loan collateral file to the note buyer, we now begin the process of boarding the loan. Boarding the loan is the act of putting the loan through your intake process. In this chapter, we will cover this intake process and discuss how it may change and evolve over time as you buy notes and gain additional experience.

The first step in boarding a loan is to input all the note information into a tracking system.

A tracking system is a key component in managing a portfolio of notes. Tracking systems can be very diverse and wide-ranging, depending on the investor's individual needs as well as the amount of notes that are being managed. For an investor that is just getting started in note investing, creating a spreadsheet file with all the pertinent loan data is more than adequate and will serve the investor well in keeping all the information organized. The scope of information includes the financial parameters of the note and details about the property, taxes and HOA fees, and the borrower. The vast majority of this data was obtained before the purchase, during the due diligence process described in chapter 5.

For investors that continue to acquire notes and grow their portfolio over time, there are other options available for tracking note information and a note portfolio. These can range from an online platform that is a server-based or cloud-hosted CRM (Customer Relationship Management) system, which has been customized to handle all the note information, to full-blown, specialized note-management platforms that are appropriate for larger investors, note fund managers, loan-servicing companies, and institutions. These loan-management platforms can easily scale and are well equipped to handle data for hundreds or thousands of notes.

At this point, the loan has been purchased, and the loan information has been entered into your tracking system. The next step is to receive and audit the physical collateral file. The collateral file is the physical folder containing all the original loan documents. This is why you might sometimes hear note investing referred to as "buying paper" by note investors.

The act of auditing the physical collateral file is an important step and must be performed immediately upon receipt of the loan file. If you recall from our earlier discussion of the loan sale agreement, there is a specified window of time in which the buyer has the ability to go back to the loan seller for recourse or for a solution to missing or incorrect loan documents, or any material defects that may be identified with the file. Keep in mind that many note sellers are handling hundreds or thousands of loan files, and from time to time, it does happen that a loan file is incomplete due to a missing mortgage assignment or missing mortgage or note. There are remedies available to correct all these situations; however, in most cases, a note seller will not sell a note when there is an issue with the collateral file. If you discover a missing document or a problem with a document in the loan file, immediately bring it to the attention of your note seller, and make sure that you do this within the period of time stated in the note sale agreement.

In the audit of the physical collateral file, you will want to make sure that the following four original documents at a minimum are contained in the file:

- **Mortgage or deed of trust.** This document should have been recorded in the county courthouse for which the property is located. If the original mortgage is ever lost, you can request a certified copy of the recorded document from the county recorder. In most cases, this will be a sufficient substitute if you ever need to enforce the lien in court. Be sure to check with your attorney if you encounter this situation.
- **Note.** This document is not recorded. If an original note document is ever lost, a copy of the note is provided along

with a lost note affidavit. In most cases, this will be a sufficient substitute if you ever need to enforce the lien in court. Be sure to check with your attorney if you encounter this situation.

- **Assignments.** A complete chain of assignments of the Assignment of Mortgage or Assignment of Deed of Trust. This means that there should be assignments for each prior owner of the note, starting with the original lender, documenting the transfer to each subsequent investor that has owned the note since its origination. These assignments need to all have been recorded in the correct order for there to be a proper chain of assignments in place. Remember that the date and time of the recording of a document dictates the order. If there is ever a missing or incorrect assignment, it will be necessary to track back to the prior note owners in order to have a new assignment document generated. There are vendors that are loan document custodians who are best at resolving these types of issues in case you ever encounter them.
- **Allonges.** Allonges or endorsements of the note, again from the original lender documenting the transfer to each subsequent investor who has owned the note since its origination. In some cases, the endorsement is stamped directly on the note document, and in other cases, the endorsement is documented by creating an allonge. An allonge is a document that is added to a note, which is used to document an endorsement of the note from the note seller to the note buyer. The same way that a check can be endorsed over to another recipient by signing the back and writing below the signature an endorsement such as "Payable to the order of [Recipient's Name]," a note can be endorsed over to a new buyer of the note. The origin of the word allonge comes from the French word allonger, which means "to lengthen."

Other documents that may be included in the file; however, these are not as important or critical:

- Title insurance policy. Useful if a title defect is discovered at any point in the future
- Original loan application
- Servicing information or records from prior loan servicer
- Lender and borrower correspondence to each other

One of the true measures of the level of skill and expertise of a note investor is the ability and comfort level to address many of the various problems that can arise with the collateral file. Having the experience and knowledge to be able to buy loans that do not have a perfect or complete collateral file is a unique skill. This is one of the ways that an investor is able to add value by acquiring a loan asset at a lower price, invest the time and effort necessary to address any collateral issues, and end up with a clean and compliant collateral file. This process will certainly increase the value of the loan and will open up many opportunities for the investor. It is very common to see loan files that have incomplete collateral or collateral issues, and many investors will simply avoid buying these loans. Investors who are able to take advantage of these opportunities will be successful negotiating a better loan purchase price and will be able to utilize their expertise to solve problems and add value to the marketplace.

THE SERVICING TRANSFER

When a note is purchased, the new owner of the note has the right to decide where the note will be serviced after the purchase has been completed. The new owner has the option to continue servicing with the prior note servicer by setting up a lender account. Alternatively, the new owner may have a relationship with another note servicer that they like, and they will prefer to initiate a servicing transfer to another servicer as provided for in the note sale agreement. Each loan servicer will have their documentation requirements and processes for initiating a servicing transfer and onboarding a loan into its servicing platform.

You may find the below steps to be somewhat familiar if the mortgage on your own property where you live (or a property that you own) has ever been sold to another lender or investor. This is a very common practice, as mortgage loans are bought and sold on the secondary market every day between lending institutions and investors.

A typical servicing transfer will consist of the following steps:

- The note buyer will provide the required documents to their loan servicer (servicer's loan setup forms, along with electronic copies of the note, the mortgage, assignments, loan modifications)
- The note seller's servicer will send a RESPA (Real Estate Settlement Procedures Act) goodbye letter to the borrower, to notify the borrower of the upcoming servicing transfer and to provide the contact information for both the old and new servicers. In addition, there are several compliance disclosures for the consumer that will be included in the body of the letter. The Real Estate Settlement Procedures Act (RESPA) regulates lenders and servicers to provide disclosures to borrowers in an effort to inform consumers in a standardized manner about real estate–related transactions.
- The note buyer's servicer will send a RESPA hello letter to the borrower, also notifying the borrower of the upcoming servicing transfer and providing the contact information for both the old and new servicers, along with the required compliance disclosures.

The RESPA letters are sent in advance of the transfer date and serve as an official handoff, or passing of the baton, with respect to loan servicing. The act of both the old and new servicer sending out similar letters with information in agreement about the loan help to document to the homeowner that the loan servicing transfer is a valid one. Homeowners are encouraged to reach out to the servicer as needed in order to confirm the transfer activity, confirm the status of the loan, or ask any other questions that they may have.

At the conclusion of the servicing transfer period, when the servicing transfer date has elapsed, the prior servicer sends an electronic data file to the new servicer containing all the loan and account information. This includes payment histories, loan information, loan balances, any outstanding amounts due, and prior servicing notes.

Moving forward, the new servicer has the loan fully boarded and is ready to service the note and receive the note payments for the account.

KEY CONCEPTS

- Immediately review your physical loan collateral file to verify that it is complete, with all the loan documents. If needed, you can engage your attorney or a loan document custodian to assist you with a collateral review.
- Your loan servicer will play a critical role during your loan purchase, in particular during the time period immediately after the loan purchase transaction occurs. Engage your servicer ahead of time, which affords you an opportunity to familiarize yourself with their servicing transfer process. Make sure you understand everything your servicer requires. This way you can be adequately prepared to provide it to them.

8

RISK MANAGEMENT

Risk is good. Not properly managing your risk is a dangerous leap.

—Evel Knievel, American stunt performer

Note investing is not without its risks, and there are numerous risks that can threaten your note, its lien position, and its value. A systematic approach to risk management will go a long way toward effectively mitigating those risks. As with most risks in life, early detection will allow for the best possible outcome with the least negative impact.

In this chapter, we will outline some of the most common and prevalent risks that are involved in note investing. It is important to get familiar with each of them and to consider your own risk tolerance. From there, you can develop your own risk management plan to be implemented and periodically fine-tuned as time goes on. Consider each of these risks and evaluate how they may (or may not) impact you based on the notes that you are choosing to invest in.

PROPERTY AND REAL ESTATE TAXES

Simply stated, real estate and property taxes must be kept current on an ongoing basis; otherwise, the ownership interest of the property and of its lien holders will quickly become threatened. Local governments and municipalities rely heavily on property tax revenue and will take quick action to enforce any delinquencies. Many homeowners have the misconception that a free and clear property (that is, free and clear of any mortgages) provides a great deal of security. However, it is always good to be reminded that if the property taxes are not paid in a timely manner, all that security will quickly vaporize once the property is taken to a tax sale. As a result, what we often will see is that for most mortgages, the lender in first position will collect a monthly escrow payment to cover the payment of property taxes and insurance, and make those payments on behalf of the borrower in order to protect the lender's interest in the property. This is something that must be established at the time of origination in the loan documents and is handled by the loan servicer. If there is no escrow for the loan, then the noteholder must verify that taxes are being paid by the homeowner in a timely manner. Payment of real estate taxes will vary significantly from county to county. It is a good idea to become very familiar with the schedules and due dates for the property taxes for each of your notes. A ten-minute phone call to the local taxing authority where the property is located will provide you with all the information you will need. If this is a task that you prefer to outsource, there are vendors that will provide a tax monitoring service for you on an ongoing basis. Tax liens placed against a property will jump ahead in priority of any mortgages. It is very important to understand that in many states, if a property is sold at a tax sale due to past delinquent taxes, the mortgage lien can be wiped out, and you will end up with an unsecured lien, which means there is no longer any collateral backing the note.

SENIOR LIENS

This risk comes into play when investing in junior position mortgages such as second-position loans. When your note is in a junior position relative to a senior lien, you must monitor the senior lien status to determine if it is current on payments. This can be verified by looking at the borrower's credit report or by contacting the senior lien holder to inquire about the loan status. It is customary that junior lien mortgage documents will include a clause stating that the lender has the right to verify that the senior lien is kept current in order to protect the lender's interest in the property.

HOMEOWNERS ASSOCIATIONS AND CONDO ASSOCIATIONS (HOA)

If the property is located within the jurisdiction of an HOA, this is another area requiring monitoring. Similar to taxes, these payments can be escrowed and handled by the loan servicer, or they can be paid by the homeowner. The handling of HOA liens and their lien positions varies significantly by law from state to state. Become knowledgeable about this topic so that you can determine how to best protect your interest in the property.

INSURANCE

Lenders typically are added to the homeowner's property insurance policy using an insurance provision called a mortgagee clause, which refers to a financial institution that has an interest in the property. This insurance provision grants special protection for the interest of the lender. In the event of a property insurance claim, the insurance company will make the check out to both the homeowner and the lender. This way, the check cannot be cashed or deposited without the endorsement (and involvement) of the lender. This protects the lender in the case of a property loss so that the insurance proceeds are actually utilized to either repair/restore the property or to pay off the lien. Lenders that are listed on the insurance policy as mortgagees will also be notified in writing about changes in the status of the policy, such as renewals, nonrenewals, or cancellations of the policy.

LOAN DEFAULTS

Loan defaults on loans that are performing are an inevitable part of the note business and something that an investor needs to be prepared to handle. It is important to maintain focus on the fact that even when the loan is in default, the mortgage loan is a secured lien and, as such, will eventually need to be addressed by the owner. During a default, the lender has several options:

- Do nothing for a limited amount of time, waiting and monitoring the loan, as many times defaults are temporary.
- Engage the loan servicer to begin loss mitigation; this would be in the form of outreach to the borrower in a manner that is ethical and compliant.
- Commence legal action (foreclosure) to enforce the lien as outlined in the mortgage documents.

Oftentimes, a loan that stops paying results from a temporary situation (such as temporary job loss or health issues), and most homeowners truly strive to have a plan to get back on track. If you encounter a default on one of your notes, work closely with both your loan servicer and your legal counsel, who will be able to step in and provide guidance and support for getting the loan back on track in a compliant manner. Foreclosing in order to enforce a lien is a process that is full of state-specific compliance requirements and legal pitfalls, and it is important that you proceed with proper guidance and that you do not undertake any actions on your own. Enforcing the lien through foreclosure is usually a last resort after all other possibilities have been exhausted. It is much more beneficial from a financial perspective to successfully negotiate an agreement or plan to get the loan back to a performing status. In the majority of all default situations the ability to achieve a resolution in which all parties benefit moving forward is generally the best outcome!

COMPLIANCE

In recent years, we have experienced a growing trend in the industry for increased regulation and regulatory enforcement for lenders and loan buyers in many states. This is an ever-changing landscape and will require constant monitoring. Become knowledgeable about compliance requirements for the states where you own notes or are planning to buy notes. Some states require licensing in order to own or to service debt. Other states have classified noteholders as debt collectors and are requiring them to obtain a debt collector license in the state. Your loan servicers and attorneys will be familiar with compliance requirements as they pertain to you, and they can provide you with valuable guidance in this area.

KEY CONCEPTS

- Risk management is an ongoing effort that will be required to protect your asset from threats. As an alternative to doing this yourself, you might consider outsourcing. There are many excellent vendors in the note industry that will provide this service to you on an ongoing basis.
- The primary areas of focus for risk management are:
    - Property taxes
    - Senior liens
    - HOA payments
    - Property insurance
    - Loan defaults
    - Regulatory compliance

9

NOTE SOURCING

WHERE CAN AN INVESTOR BUY NOTES?

You can get everything in life you want if
you will just help enough other people get what they want.

—Zig Ziglar, American author and motivational speaker

Networking is not about just connecting people.
It's about connecting people with people, people with ideas,
and people with opportunities.

—Michele Jennae, author

Note investing is very much a relationship-based business, and nowhere is that more prevalent than in the realm of sourcing available notes to buy. For many, this is one of the most challenging areas of the notes business. I am often asked the same question by newer investors: "I am looking for notes. Where do I go to buy notes? I cannot seem to find any." It truly does take constant outreach and effort to be successful at finding notes to buy. We will discuss some of the more popular avenues for sourcing notes here in this chapter.

The first, and what might be the obvious, choice might be to buy notes directly from a bank. However, this presents quite a challenge with significant barriers to entry. In most cases, the well-known large, nationwide banks in the United States do not typically sell notes to individual investors. These banks will sell their loans to other financial institutions in very large trades, involving thousands of notes and many millions of dollars in a single transaction. This is not typically a space for the individual investor to be transacting in, and you would be hard pressed to even be able to speak with someone working at the institution that is even remotely associated with sales of notes.

For the individual investor seeking to purchase notes, they would be much better served by exploring some of the possibilities described below.

Building your network of contacts of other note investors and note funds that operate in this space will often yield the best results. Developing your networking and relationship skills and getting out to note events and note-investing conferences will place you directly in environments that are full of note sellers and note buyers, and provide you ample opportunities to buy notes. Those relationships, which are built over time with constant effort, will be a sure way to provide access to notes for purchase.

NOTE FUNDS

Note funds that are in the business of buying notes in larger quantities will often also sell notes on a somewhat regular basis. Some note funds will be winding down (typically at the end of the calendar year) and will be looking to sell some or all of their notes. Through your relationships with the fund managers, you will be able to stay abreast of these opportunities so that you can position yourself to be in the right place at the right time.

ONLINE NOTE EXCHANGES

Online exchanges that exist for buyers and sellers of notes to do transactions are becoming more prevalent in the notes industry. Some of the exchanges even serve in the capacity of a neutral closing agent between seller and buyer, which will help to insure a good, clean transaction between the two parties.

NOTE CONFERENCES AND EVENTS

There are any number of note conferences that are regularly held around the country, where hundreds of note sellers, buyers, and vendors come together. Seek out these events and make an effort to attend and meet your colleagues in the note industry as often as possible.

NOTE SERVICERS

Note servicers handle many thousands of notes for their clients, and it really does pay off to develop personal relationships with your contacts at the note servicers. Note servicers will often be the first to know when an investor who is their customer will be preparing to sell off notes or to liquidate a large note portfolio and sometimes may be able to facilitate an introduction.

INDIVIDUAL NOTE INVESTORS

Network, network, and network! Today there are so many options available for networking, either through online investing communities or at in-person events, national conferences, and local or regional meetings. Over time, you will get to know the people that are active in this industry, and you will develop a good contact list. Staying in touch regularly will help to keep you top of mind when someone has a note that they are looking to sell.

Exploring these avenues for potential sales of notes will certainly yield results. An approach that is focused around constant and consistent outreach will usually be the best and most effective strategy. Utilizing technology tools such as a digital calendar or CRM (Customer Relationship Management) system to manage the proactive outreach can prove to be very effective for note investors.

KEY CONCEPTS

- Finding where to source notes is hard work. You must develop skills such as the ability to build relationships and effective person-to-person networking, and you must implement a system for consistent outreach. Combining those skills with continuous, focused effort over the long term will yield the best results.

10

BUYING NOTES INSIDE A SELF-DIRECTED ACCOUNT

Control your own destiny or someone else will.

—Jack Welch, former CEO, General Electric

Buying a note inside your self-directed IRA account is one of the most powerful note investing strategies that can be put into action. (For a detailed discussion of self-directed accounts, please see chapter 11.) As we discussed previously, note investing is a business activity that, although it can be very profitable, can often result in a significant tax burden for the investor. This will typically appear in the form of capital gains and interest income.

By combining note investing with tax-advantaged accounts, the tax burdens can be minimized to a large extent, particularly when using a self-directed Roth IRA. In this case, no taxes will be due on the gains from the investment activity (the profits derived from the note).

The self-directed account should be considered a bucket, or a financial vehicle, in which to own assets. These assets can be acquired, grown, and held inside the self-directed account as part of an overall long-term investment strategy.

In order to maintain the account in compliance with IRS rules, consider the self-directed account to always maintain an arm's length from the account holder during all transactions.

The mechanics of a note purchase in a self-directed account are fairly straightforward. All transactions in your self-directed account are executed on your behalf, according to your instructions, by the account custodian. The role of the account custodian is to maintain the account, to facilitate transactions, and to make sure that the account holder is not entering into any prohibited transactions. The custodian is not permitted to recommend or give any opinion or advice about an investment.

The following is a high-level overview of the purchase process:

- The investor finds and negotiates a note to be purchased in the self-directed account and conducts due diligence on the note.

- The investor fills out and prepares the self-directed custodian's asset purchase forms and instructions.
- The note purchase agreement is prepared between the seller and buyer. The buyer named in the purchase agreement will be the investor's IRA account.
- The custodian will sign the agreement on behalf of the IRA.
- The custodian will draw the purchase money against the IRA account and send it to the note seller to fund the transaction.
- The note seller will generate an assignment of mortgage to the IRA as the new owner and transfer ownership of the note to the IRA.
- All subsequent payments received on the note will be sent to the IRA custodian and will be placed into the IRA account.

That is what takes place for purchasing a note in your IRA. The selling of a note that is owned by an IRA is a very similar process.

Here are some additional observations to keep in mind.

Other than the activities of finding the note, negotiating the purchase, and conducting due diligence, the account holder was not involved directly in the asset purchase. In fact, those activities were conducted prior to the actual purchase closing.

The custodian handled all of the transactional aspects of the purchase, and in particular, the handling of the funds. At no point is the account holder permitted to take direct possession of IRA funds; otherwise, it would be considered a taxable distribution and subject to taxes and penalties.

The note is titled in the name of the IRA, and all payments or proceeds from that note are to be sent directly into the IRA.

Any expenses related to the note, such as servicing fees, recording fees, legal work, and so on, must be paid for by the custodian on your behalf from funds in the self-directed account.

Absolutely *do not* comingle funds by paying for expenses out of a personal or business account.

Once the investor is familiar with the rules and details of how to handle note transactions in an IRA and how to coordinate with their custodian, this process becomes second nature. Note investors are encouraged to utilize this strategy as often as reasonably possible, as it is an extremely powerful strategy that contributes to long-term growth.

CASE STUDY: DELTONA, FLORIDA

This note was a performing second-position mortgage with 174 remaining payments on a residential property located in Central Florida. There was a portion of the note that was a balloon payment, meaning that there was an amount due at the end of the term that was carved out and was not accumulating interest like the rest of the principal balance. In most cases, a balloon payment benefits the borrower by lowering their monthly payment but adds additional risk exposure at note maturity (as the balloon payment is due in full at note maturity) and does not significantly increase the value of the note to an investor. The additional risk to consider is that when the balloon payment becomes due at that future date, will the borrower have enough funds to make this large payment at one time? However, if the property is ever sold or refinanced, then the balloon payment will be paid at closing, out of the proceeds of that financial transaction.

This note had a good payment history, and the owner of the note was selling it in order to raise capital for another investment opportunity.

NOTE DETAILS

Monthly payment amount = $420.95

Remaining payments = 174

Interest rate = 12%

Principal balance = $34,716

Deferred balloon payment (due at loan maturity) = $7,659.61

TRANSACTION DETAILS

Note purchase price = $31,000

Rate of return = 14.2% per year

We elected to purchase this note and own it inside our self-directed Roth IRA account. This was a good investment in the Roth account, earning approximately a 14% rate of return with monthly payments of $420.95. As a result of buying this note at a discount, this has effectively increased the rate of return from 12% to 14.2%. The fact that this was being held in a Roth IRA account meant that there would be absolutely no tax due on any of the income or gains from this investment.

This note was held for thirteen months, and then suddenly our loan servicer received a payoff request from the borrower. The property was being sold, and the title company handling the closing sent in a wire transfer to the loan servicer for the full amount due, which included the remaining principal balance plus the deferred balloon payment. When all was said and done, we had received thirteen monthly payments of $420.95 plus the payoff amount of $41,878.61.

This is an excellent opportunity for us to lean in deeper to the analysis and calculate the actual rate of return on this investment. Because the loan was paid off in full earlier than expected, we received what is known as "uneven cash flows" and realized a rate of return significantly higher than the expected 14.2% per year.

There is a very useful function in Microsoft Excel, XIRR, which calculates the internal rate of return for a series of cash flows that occur at irregular intervals or irregular amounts. Using this function, we can make up a quick spreadsheet in order to calculate the internal rate of return. In this spreadsheet, I have entered in all the cash inflows (the payments received expressed as positive numbers) and cash outflows (the initial funding for the investment expressed as a negative number) along with the dates of each payment (in chronological order).

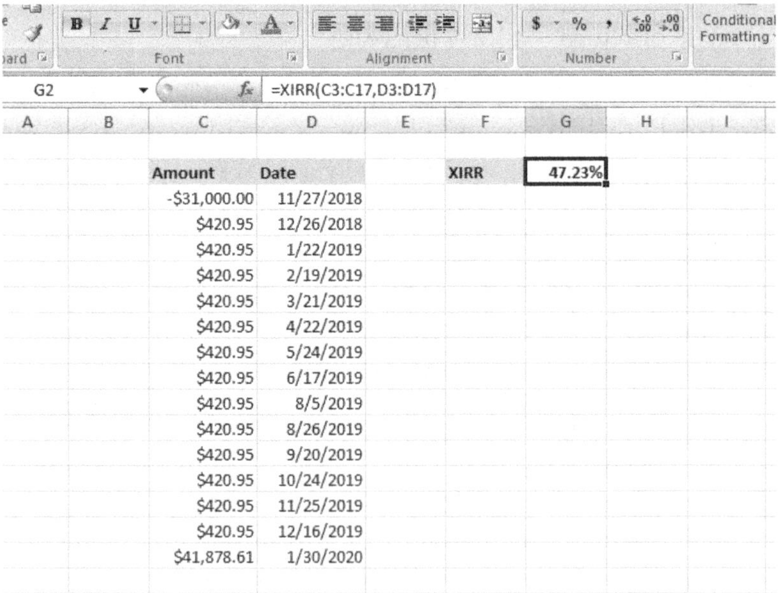

Amount	Date
-$31,000.00	11/27/2018
$420.95	12/26/2018
$420.95	1/22/2019
$420.95	2/19/2019
$420.95	3/21/2019
$420.95	4/22/2019
$420.95	5/24/2019
$420.95	6/17/2019
$420.95	8/5/2019
$420.95	8/26/2019
$420.95	9/20/2019
$420.95	10/24/2019
$420.95	11/25/2019
$420.95	12/16/2019
$41,878.61	1/30/2020

FIGURE 10.1. USING EXCEL'S XIRR FUNCTION TO CALCULATE INTERNAL RATE OF RETURN.

FINAL RESULTS

Investment amount (loan purchase price) = $31,000

Total monthly payments received: $420.95 × 13 = $5,472.35

Total received from loan payoff = $41,878.61

Grand total = $47,350.96

Internal rate of return = 47%

KEY CONCEPTS

- Holding notes as assets owned inside a retirement account can prove to be an extremely powerful combination due to the tax-advantaged treatment.
- Always consult with your CPA or tax attorney to determine if the strategy using self-directed accounts would be appropriate for your own particular situation.
- Your self-directed custodian is a major partner on your team. Work closely with your custodian to become educated and fully understand the IRS rules and operational details involved with your type of account.

11

THE POWER OF SELF-DIRECTED ACCOUNTS

IRAS, ROTH IRAS, HSAS, ESAS, AND HOW THEY ARE IDEAL FOR HOLDING NOTE INVESTMENTS

Over and over again, courts have said there is nothing sinister
in so arranging one's affairs as to keep taxes as low as possible.
Everybody does so, rich and poor, and all do right,
for nobody owes any public duty to pay more than the law demands.
Taxes are enforced exactions, not voluntary contributions.

—Honorable Learned Hand, US Appeals Court Justice

As we learned in the previous chapter, self-directed accounts are ideal vehicles for investing in notes, particularly due to the tax treatment they are granted. Note investing is an activity that results in high rates of return, and in most cases, this will generate a tax liability for the investor. If note investing is done inside a self-directed IRA account, the preferential tax treatment inside the account will significantly boost the results and the financial growth that is occurring.

Self-directed accounts are a specific type of account that allows you to save (for retirement, health expenses, or education expenses) on a tax-advantaged basis, and it has the same eligibility and contribution rules as its traditional counterparts. Self-directed accounts allow you to do exactly what the name describes, which is to allow *you* to direct the types of investments in which to invest. With traditional retirement accounts and employer 401(k) plans offered by the mega banking and investment institutions, the custodians will limit you to only being able to invest in the typical market-traded investment products, such as stocks, bonds, and mutual funds (remember that these are all products for which the financial institutions earn a commission when selling to you). With self-directing custodians, the options really open up to you and provide you with the flexibility to invest in alternative investments, such as real estate, mortgages and notes, business loans and leases, private investment funds, or even sporting event tickets.

Are self-directed accounts legal? Yes, they absolutely are, and the US Internal Revenue Service even has a publication on the topic, called IRS Publication 590. Self-directed accounts can be any of the following types of accounts: IRA, Roth IRA, 401(k), Roth 401(k), pension plan, SEP, HSA, or Coverdell account. For the purposes of our discussion, the term *IRA* or *self-directed IRA* may be used to refer to any type of the previously mentioned tax-advantaged accounts.

This is such a powerful strategy, one that Wall Street does not want you to know about. Your traditional financial advisors and brokerage house custodians have a vested interest in continuing to collect fees and commissions from the financial services and products that they offer to their customers. This is why they will steer you in the direction of the Wall Street products instead of the self-directed realm.

Based on the current IRS rules, there is not a list of approved or allowed investments for IRA accounts. Instead, there is only a list of investments that are *not* allowed:

- Life insurance
- Jewelry (however, precious metals themselves in certain forms are allowed)
- Collectibles (art, antiques, stamps, coins, alcoholic beverages)
- Prohibited transactions (transactions done with yourself or with a disqualified person)

IRS rules prohibit the self-directed account from dealing with parties that are disqualified persons, which include yourself and your spouse, members of your family that are lineal descendants (parents, children, grandparents, grandchildren), and their spouses. Also, persons who are acting in a fiduciary capacity, such as a CPA, attorney, financial planner, and so on may be considered disqualified persons, depending on their relationship with the self-directed account owner. The IRS has made it clear that any disqualified persons must remain at arm's length from any self-directed account transactions. Disqualified persons may not buy or sell any asset from the IRA, may not do business with an asset in the IRA, may not live in or rent an asset in the IRA (in the case of a rental property), or make a commission or be paid for any service being provided to the IRA.

Another type of prohibited transaction to be mindful of is to avoid self-dealing, which is directly borrowing money from the IRA, comingling of funds from other taxable accounts, selling assets to it, or furnishing services to it. All transactions must be conducted at arm's length and must utilize third-party vendors or service providers as needed. Your self-directed custodian is typically well versed in all transactions and can provide beneficial guidance for keeping your self-directed account in compliance with the IRS prohibited transaction rules.

For the investments that you make in a self-directed account, the responsibility for due diligence is completely on you (stressing the word "self" in self-directed) to perform thoroughly. It is important that you fully understand the investments you are making in the self-directed account, as the custodian is not permitted to provide any financial, tax, or legal advice regarding the investments. Also, custodians are not permitted to recommend any specific investments for their account holders. This underscores the importance of leveraging your professional advisors (CPA, attorney, etc.) for providing this support.

MY OWN EXPERIENCE

I have been utilizing self-directed accounts for well over a decade and have benefited tremendously from their flexibility. This has allowed me to consistently earn above-average returns on investments such as:

- A private stock offering in a local community bank that was raising capital as a start-up
- Large real estate, multifamily apartment deals (real estate syndications)
- Buying and holding real estate mortgage notes and note partials
- Investing in note funds and joint ventures related to notes
- Partial ownership interest in an oil and gas lease

The self-direction aspect of the account means that I am solely responsible to find, evaluate, and make or perform (indirectly) the asset in which the capital has been invested. It is self-accountability in the highest sense of the phrase. This allows me to invest in what I truly know and understand, and to leverage the knowledge that I (or my investment partners) have in this area. You can see that having these assets as a component of my overall portfolio protects the portfolio against stock market volatility and fluctuation.

Self-directed IRAs allow you to receive the tax benefits of a retirement account but allow you to invest in assets that can have a much greater profit potential than what is typical of a stock, bond, or mutual fund.

As an example, I have a friend, James, who is a medical professional and is a high wage earner in a high tax bracket. He contributes annually to his self-directed IRA, and inside that account, he has purchased a partial ownership interest in a 550-unit apartment building in Texas. The building is professionally managed and owned together with other owners, and the investment sponsors are the ones that actually operate the property and make it a hands-off investment for James. The property generates monthly rent and dividend payments, which are sent directly back into James's account each month. James is busy focusing on his successful medical career, and he does not have time for, nor does he want to, have anything to do with operating the apartment building. It is truly a passive investment, and he is able to participate financially and reap the benefits of ownership.

TAKE ME OUT TO THE BALL GAME

Here is one of my favorite and most creative stories about self-directed investments. I have a friend, Malcolm, who used his self-directed account to buy a seat license at the stadium of our local professional football team. With this seat license, he was guaranteed tickets ahead of time for the entire sports season each year. While it would have been a prohibited transaction for him to use the tickets himself, he would sell the tickets at a profit out of his self-directed account using an online ticket-selling portal and then have the proceeds of the sales go right back into his self-directed account.

A final point I would like to emphasize is that self-directing presents a unique opportunity to anyone who possesses a specialized skill set, whether that be in a hobby, a technology, or a business sector. This places them in a position to be able to analyze an investment opportunity through the lens of their specialized knowledge and expertise. This all comes back to the concept of investing in what you know:

- A surgeon who constantly follows medical breakthroughs and invests in pharmaceutical start-ups involved in developing a new lifesaving treatment or technology
- A real estate developer or builder who learns about new construction products and materials and invests in companies that produce these items
- A computer network architect that encounters growing trends in his field and invests in start-up opportunities with relevant technology companies that have private stock offerings
- A real estate investor who watches the real estate market cycles and invests in large real estate syndications
- A media industry veteran who watches the explosive trends in podcasting as a major industry disruption and decides to invest in a friend's private offering into a podcast production company

In particular, if you have specialized knowledge about a particular technology or business sector, you are very well equipped to utilize your unique skills to analyze and evaluate an investment opportunity that presents itself to you.

TAX-ADVANTAGED ACCOUNTS EXPLAINED AT A GLANCE

401(k) or Traditional IRA

- Start contributing consistently when you are young. Even fifty or a hundred dollars a month will make a big impact over time.
- Try to take maximum advantage of 401(k) employer matching programs.
- You receive a tax deduction on your contributions; however, when funds are withdrawn during retirement years, you will pay taxes on withdrawals.
- You will pay taxes on all growth realized in the account over the years.
- You are paying taxes on the harvest, not on the seed.

Roth 401(k) or Roth IRA

- No tax deduction on contributions; however, withdrawals after growth will not be subject to any tax.
- You are paying taxes only on the seed, not on the harvest.
- Growth in the account is not subject to taxes. You are paying taxes on the dollars that are contributed into the account. No taxes are due when funds are withdrawn during retirement years. Because of the favored tax treatment, these accounts allow for significantly better growth over traditional 401(k) or traditional IRA accounts.

HSA (Health Savings Account)

- Tax deduction on contributions.
- Withdrawals/reimbursements for health-related expenses are not subject to tax.
- Growth in the account is not subject to taxes. No taxes paid on the seed; no taxes paid on the harvest.

- Reimbursements may be deferred as long as you like and do not need to happen in the year the expense was incurred. The strategy with HSAs is to keep deferring your reimbursements for many years out into the future, allowing the account to grow significantly. Then, in the future, after there is a critical mass of assets and income in the account, you can begin to reimburse yourself for those qualified expenses.

Coverdell Education Savings Account (ESA)

- No tax deduction on contributions.
- Earnings growth is tax free and withdrawals are tax free when utilized for qualified education expenses.
- You are paying taxes only on the seed, not on the harvest.

A FUNNY THING HAPPENED ON THE WAY TO WORK TODAY

Ken grew up in the United States, the son of a first-generation immigrant. His father had immigrated to America from India as a young man, and he spent most of his career working long hours on the trading floor of the New York Stock Exchange. Ken grew up watching his father work very hard to provide for the family; however, he always had a sadness as he noticed the constant struggle in the family with finances. Ken's father was very much of the traditional mindset to work very hard and save as best he could. You see, unfortunately for him, he got sold on the story about getting good grades, finding a good job, working hard, saving money, and investing blindly in his employer's retirement plan. That retirement plan consisted of what we often see, which is the half dozen or so Wall Street options that are routinely offered in 401(k) plans.

As Ken became an adult and started to become more independent, he was successful in his professional career and was busy raising his own family. Ken watched his father transition into retirement, and he became deeply troubled watching as his father continued to struggle financially despite all his father had saved and invested during his working years.

Ken continued to work, and he was contributing to his employer 401(k) plan consistently. At the end of the year, Ken was looking over his annual account statement and was shocked and dismayed when he observed that the account balance over the past year had increased only by the same amount he had contributed. He felt a sinking feeling in his stomach as he began questioning, "Why did the account balance not increase this year as the markets did? The stock market has been doing fairly well! What happened to all the return on my investments?"

At that moment, Ken resolved that he was not going to go down the same financial path as his father. The thought of him potentially making those same mistakes was quite painful. He knew that the financial future of his family was depending on him taking action and making better choices. Ken decided that he would take an active role in learning how to manage his investments. Ken began to study personal finance and investing, and he learned about different alternative investment asset classes, strategies, and opportunities that were not the traditional Wall Street options. He was pleased to find that there was an abundance of educational information available through books, podcasts, investment conferences, and finance blogs. He started to study and learn more about investing in real estate, notes and mortgages, and other alternatives. Ken ended up investing in several real estate deals and a note fund, all using capital from his retirement account.

This way of investing seemed very appealing to him, he was excited about moving forward, and he felt extremely comfortable knowing that he was heading down a better path. Within the span of several months, Ken went through a dramatic transformation: he went from dreading opening his quarterly retirement account statement to actually being excited to open the account statement and see the recurring cash flow payments being deposited into the account.

KEY CONCEPTS

- Self-directed accounts allow the account holder to self-direct, which means the account holder is able to make an investment choice and then issue a directive to the custodian to disburse the funds into that investment.
- Through the use of self-directed accounts, we are able to deploy retirement account funds into many types of alternative investment asset classes, such as real estate, private equity for businesses that are not publicly traded (such as small businesses and start-ups), and notes.
- Self-directing allows a person to invest in what they know. In particular, if you have specialized knowledge about a particular technology or business sector, you are very well equipped to utilize your unique skills to analyze and evaluate an investment opportunity that presents itself to you.
- Although self-directed accounts are not widely known, they are perfectly legal. If you would like to read further about the tax code provisions for retirement accounts, see IRS Publication 590.
- The IRS does not provide a list of approved or allowed investments for IRA accounts. Instead, there is only a list of investments that are prohibited. This means that anything else is allowed.

12

INVESTING IN PARTIALS

INSTEAD OF BUYING THE WHOLE PIZZA, WHY NOT JUST BUY A SLICE?

Half a loaf is better than none.

—John Heywood, English author and playwright

Partials are a unique strategy and a rather interesting tool that can be part of your note investing toolbox. By now, we are very familiar with the idea that a note can be sold, with all the remaining payments being transferred to the note buyer. With a partial, there is only part of the note being sold, in other words, the sale of only part of the payments. This part can be any amount of the future payments, for example, one year, five years, or even twenty years of payments. The number of payments contained in the partial can be anything that is agreed to between the seller and buyer. The seller retains the back end of the note (which consists of the balance of the remaining payments on the term of the note), and once the duration of the partial has ended, then the payment stream automatically reverts back to the seller of the partial for the duration of those remaining payments.

Why would someone want to sell or buy just part of a note? Partials can be a very powerful technique in that they offer an extreme amount of flexibility to both the seller and buyer. The noteholder might need to raise a small amount of cash quickly and might not wish to sell the entire note. If they were to sell a partial, they could sell only the number of payments necessary to raise the specific amount of cash that they need. This way, any discount that the seller would need to offer is minimized. Or, alternatively, a buyer may not have enough capital to purchase the entire note, so instead, they buy a partial using the funds that they have available to spend. This allows the noteholder to sell a smaller quantity of payments, and then retain the remaining number of payments that are due on the note. This provides the noteholder with needed liquidity while continuing to retain an ownership interest in the investment. For example, there could be a note with twenty years of payments remaining, and the noteholder sells a partial consisting of five years' worth of payments. The partial buyer purchases the partial of five years of payments and receives that payment stream for sixty months. Then, starting in month sixty-one, the payment stream reverts back to the noteholder, and they receive the remaining payments due on the note from years six through twenty.

Let's illustrate the concept of partials using this following example: if we have a note that was originated with a principal balance of $100,000 at 6% interest for a term of thirty years (360 payments), the monthly payment works out to have a payment amount of $599.55.

A partial is sold consisting of five years of payments (sixty monthly payments) to an investor. The buyer of the partial has negotiated a discounted price of $29,569.36, and if we calculate the rate of return for sixty payments at this discounted price, that works out to an annual return rate of 8%. The buyer of the partial will receive their sixty monthly payments, which will total $35,973.60 in principal and interest payments over the life of the partial.

In month sixty-one, the partial has ended, and the payment stream reverts back to the note seller with the remaining principal balance of the note of $93,054.37. The note seller still owns the back end of the note and will receive the remaining three hundred monthly payments. This transition of the payment stream is coordinated by the note servicer. This way, the borrower on the note is not impacted in any way by the details of this partial sale.

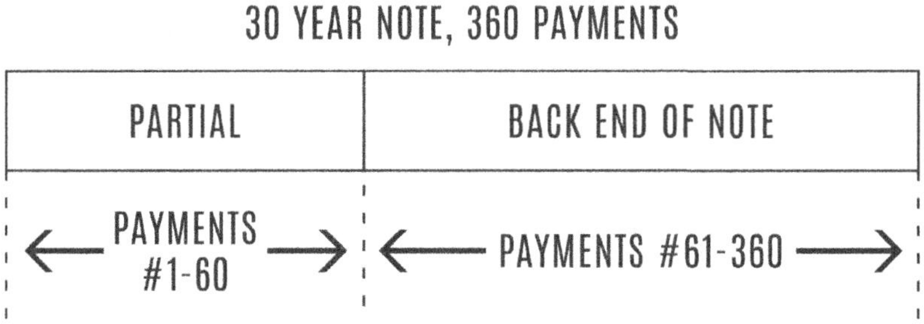

FIGURE 12.1. A NOTE PARTIAL IS JUST PART OF A NOTE!

When a noteholder sells a partial to another investor, the noteholder is still retaining the back end, or the tail end, of that payment stream. Therefore, the noteholder continues to have a vested interest in the overall success of the note after they have sold off the partial. Now, the partial buyer of course is investing their hard-earned capital, and they also have a vested interest in the overall success of the note. With this business transaction, we can clearly see that the ongoing interests of both the note seller and the partial buyer are congruent. This results in an overall collaborative effort in which both parties work together to insure a successful outcome if any risks or problems were ever to arise.

Here are some important points to keep in mind when dealing with partials.

NOTE ACCOUNTING AND AMORTIZATION SCHEDULE

Accounting on a partial can become quite complex, and it is best to leave this to the experts. You absolutely want to make sure that your loan servicer is set up to handle partials with their software and systems. Be sure to ask detailed questions about this up front to make sure that you are comfortable with the servicer's ability to handle partials on a note.

On a note with a partial, there will be two separate amortization schedules that will run in parallel. One schedule for the note and its original term, and then an amortization schedule for the partial. Each schedule will track the current principal balance along with how much of each payment is being allocated between principal and interest.

WHAT HAPPENS IF THERE IS AN EARLY PAYOFF ON THE NOTE?

If there is a loan payoff that takes place at any time, the holder of the partial will be paid first, followed by payment to the holder of the back end of the note. The loan servicer will calculate the payout of the remaining principal balance owed on the partial at the date of the payoff. The servicer will also calculate the payout of the remaining principal balance owed on the remaining term of the loan.

WHAT HAPPENS IN THE CASE OF A DEFAULT DURING THE PARTIAL?

If the note goes into default, the partial agreement will define exactly the options in place. Most often in these agreements, the holder of the partial has the full right to enforce the lien in order to recover their investment capital (if they wish). The partial holder may sometimes prefer to defer this right to the note seller and allow them to enforce the lien, particularly if the partial holder is not experienced with the legal process or if they do not wish to invest additional time or capital in order to bring about a resolution. If the lien is enforced and the property is foreclosed, the sale proceeds will pay off the partial holder first, and then any remaining amount will go to pay off the investor holding the back end of the note. The important point is that the partial holder has priority and will be paid off first, followed by the investor holding the back end of the note.

WHAT HAPPENS WHEN THE TERM OF THE PARTIAL RUNS OUT?

When the term of the partial has ended, there is no impact to the borrower paying on the note. The note servicer should stop forwarding payments to the partial holder, as they are exiting from the deal, and should begin forwarding payments to the investor holding the back end of the note. If everything is done properly and according to plan, this should result in a seamless transaction for all parties involved. Of course, a common occurrence is that the partial holder had gotten used to receiving that cash flow stream each month, and now that it has ended, they certainly might approach the noteholder again to buy a new partial on that same note.

Partials are a powerful tool used to customize a very flexible solution to meet the needs of both the buyer and seller. Partials are also very beneficial to a note buyer by allowing them to buy into a note with a smaller amount of capital while realizing most of the same benefits of owning the whole note.

CASE STUDY: DEERFIELD BEACH, FLORIDA

This was a performing second-position mortgage with a thirty-year term (360 payments) on a residential property located in South Florida. The note had a good, consistent payment history for the past several years, and the holder of the note was seeking to sell a partial in order to recapitalize part of their investment. We bought a partial on this note, which consisted of purchasing a payment stream of the next seventy-seven payments of $295.25 per month.

DETAILS OF THE PARTIAL

Partial purchase price = $15,000

Payment = $295.25

Remaining payments = 77

Principal balance = $15,000

Rate of return = 13.78%

DETAILS OF THE UNDERLYING NOTE

Interest rate = 5%

Remaining payments = 341

Principal balance = $53,767.44

When computing a partial, there are actually two parallel amortization tables that run concurrently, one for the partial and one for the underlying note. Let's take a deeper dive into this partial by looking at the following table. This illustrates all the details and will help you better understand what is happening with the partial along with its relationship to the underlying note.

DATE	PARTIAL PMT #	PMT #	PAYMENT	INTEREST	PRINCIPAL	PARTIAL PAYOFF	NOTE BALANCE
						$15,000.00	$53,767.44
7/1/18	1	341	$295.25	$173.38	$121.87	$14,878.13	$53,696.22
8/1/18	2	340	$295.25	$171.97	$123.28	$14,754.85	$53,624.70
9/1/18	3	339	$295.25	$170.54	$124.71	$14,630.14	$53,552.89
10/1/18	4	338	$295.25	$169.10	$126.15	$14,503.99	$53,480.78
11/1/18	5	337	$295.25	$167.64	$127.61	$14,376.38	$53,408.37
12/1/18	6	336	$295.25	$166.17	$129.08	$14,247.30	$53,335.65
1/1/19	7	335	$295.25	$164.68	$130.57	$14,116.73	$53,262.63
2/1/19	8	334	$295.25	$163.17	$132.08	$13,984.65	$53,189.31
3/1/19	9	333	$295.25	$161.64	$133.61	$13,851.04	$53,115.68
4/1/19	10	332	$295.25	$160.09	$135.16	$13,715.88	$53,041.75
5/1/19	11	331	$295.25	$158.53	$136.72	$13,579.16	$52,967.51
6/1/19	12	330	$295.25	$156.95	$138.30	$13,440.86	$52,892.96
7/1/19	13	329	$295.25	$155.35	$139.90	$13,300.96	$52,818.10
8/1/19	14	328	$295.25	$153.74	$141.51	$13,159.45	$52,742.93
9/1/19	15	327	$295.25	$152.10	$143.15	$13,016.30	$52,667.44
10/1/19	16	326	$295.25	$150.45	$144.80	$12,871.50	$52,591.64
11/1/19	17	325	$295.25	$148.77	$146.48	$12,725.02	$52,515.52
12/1/19	18	324	$295.25	$147.08	$148.17	$12,576.85	$52,439.08
1/1/20	19	323	$295.25	$145.37	$149.88	$12,426.97	$52,362.33
2/1/20	20	322	$295.25	$143.64	$151.61	$12,275.36	$52,285.26
3/1/20	21	321	$295.25	$141.88	$153.37	$12,121.99	$52,207.87
4/1/20	22	320	$295.25	$140.11	$155.14	$11,966.85	$52,130.15

DATE	PARTIAL PMT #	PMT #	PAYMENT	INTEREST	PRINCIPAL	PARTIAL PAYOFF	NOTE BALANCE
5/1/20	23	319	$295.25	$138.32	$156.93	$11,809.92	$52,052.11
6/1/20	24	318	$295.25	$136.50	$158.75	$11,651.17	$51,973.74
7/1/20	25	317	$295.25	$134.67	$160.58	$11,490.59	$51,895.05
8/1/20	26	316	$295.25	$132.81	$162.44	$11,328.15	$51,816.03
9/1/20	27	315	$295.25	$130.93	$164.32	$11,163.83	$51,736.68
10/1/20	28	314	$295.25	$129.04	$166.21	$10,997.62	$51,657.00
11/1/20	29	313	$295.25	$127.11	$168.14	$10,829.48	$51,576.99
12/1/20	30	312	$295.25	$125.17	$170.08	$10,659.40	$51,496.64
1/1/21	31	311	$295.25	$123.20	$172.05	$10,487.35	$51,415.96
2/1/21	32	310	$295.25	$121.22	$174.03	$10,313.32	$51,334.94
3/1/21	33	309	$295.25	$119.20	$176.05	$10,137.27	$51,253.59
4/1/21	34	308	$295.25	$117.17	$178.08	$9,959.19	$51,171.90
5/1/21	35	307	$295.25	$115.11	$180.14	$9,779.05	$51,089.87
6/1/21	36	306	$295.25	$113.03	$182.22	$9,596.83	$51,007.49
7/1/21	37	305	$295.25	$110.92	$184.33	$9,412.50	$50,924.77
8/1/21	38	304	$295.25	$108.79	$186.46	$9,226.04	$50,841.71
9/1/21	39	303	$295.25	$106.64	$188.61	$9,037.43	$50,758.30
10/1/21	40	302	$295.25	$104.46	$190.79	$8,846.64	$50,674.54
11/1/21	41	301	$295.25	$102.25	$193.00	$8,653.64	$50,590.43
12/1/21	42	300	$295.25	$100.02	$195.23	$8,458.41	$50,505.97
1/1/22	43	299	$295.25	$97.77	$197.48	$8,260.93	$50,421.16
2/1/22	44	298	$295.25	$95.48	$199.77	$8,061.16	$50,336.00
3/1/22	45	297	$295.25	$93.17	$202.08	$7,859.08	$50,250.48
4/1/22	46	296	$295.25	$90.84	$204.41	$7,654.67	$50,164.61
5/1/22	47	295	$295.25	$88.48	$206.77	$7,447.90	$50,078.38
6/1/22	48	294	$295.25	$86.09	$209.16	$7,238.74	$49,991.79
7/1/22	49	293	$295.25	$83.67	$211.58	$7,027.16	$49,904.84
8/1/22	50	292	$295.25	$81.22	$214.03	$6,813.13	$49,817.53
9/1/22	51	291	$295.25	$78.75	$216.50	$6,596.63	$49,729.85
10/1/22	52	290	$295.25	$76.25	$219.00	$6,377.63	$49,641.81
11/1/22	53	289	$295.25	$73.71	$221.54	$6,156.09	$49,553.40
12/1/22	54	288	$295.25	$71.15	$224.10	$5,931.99	$49,464.62
1/1/23	55	287	$295.25	$68.56	$226.69	$5,705.30	$49,375.47
2/1/23	56	286	$295.25	$65.94	$229.31	$5,475.99	$49,285.95
3/1/23	57	285	$295.25	$63.29	$231.96	$5,244.03	$49,196.06
4/1/23	58	284	$295.25	$60.61	$234.64	$5,009.39	$49,105.79
5/1/23	59	283	$295.25	$57.90	$237.35	$4,772.04	$49,015.15

DATE	PARTIAL PMT #	PMT #	PAYMENT	INTEREST	PRINCIPAL	PARTIAL PAYOFF	NOTE BALANCE
6/1/23	60	282	$295.25	$55.16	$240.09	$4,531.95	$48,924.13
7/1/23	61	281	$295.25	$52.38	$242.87	$4,289.08	$48,832.73
8/1/23	62	280	$295.25	$49.57	$245.68	$4,043.40	$48,740.95
9/1/23	63	279	$295.25	$46.73	$248.52	$3,794.88	$48,648.79
10/1/23	64	278	$295.25	$43.86	$251.39	$3,543.49	$48,556.24
11/1/23	65	277	$295.25	$40.96	$254.29	$3,289.20	$48,463.31
12/1/23	66	276	$295.25	$38.02	$257.23	$3,031.97	$48,369.99
1/1/24	67	275	$295.25	$35.04	$260.21	$2,771.76	$48,276.28
2/1/24	68	274	$295.25	$32.04	$263.21	$2,508.55	$48,182.18
3/1/24	69	273	$295.25	$28.99	$266.26	$2,242.29	$48,087.69
4/1/24	70	272	$295.25	$25.92	$269.33	$1,972.96	$47,992.81
5/1/24	71	271	$295.25	$22.80	$272.45	$1,700.51	$47,897.53
6/1/24	72	270	$295.25	$19.66	$275.59	$1,424.92	$47,801.85
7/1/24	73	269	$295.25	$16.47	$278.78	$1,146.14	$47,705.77
8/1/24	74	268	$295.25	$13.25	$282.00	$864.14	$47,609.29
9/1/24	75	267	$295.25	$9.99	$285.26	$578.88	$47,512.41
10/1/24	76	266	$295.25	$6.69	$288.56	$290.32	$47,415.13
11/1/24	77	265	$295.25	$6.50	$290.32	$0.00	$47,317.44
TOTALS			**$22,734.25**	**$7,735.82**	**$15,000.00**	**$0.00**	

The columns from left to right display the following information:

- **Date.** This is the monthly payment due date for each payment.
- **Payment #.** Each partial payment, showing the seventy-seven monthly payments that make up this partial.
- **Term Left.** This is the term of the underlying 360-month note. For the purposes of this partial, we are looking at monthly payments counting down from 341 to 265 on that note, which identifies the payment stream that was purchased.
- **Payment.** This is the monthly payment of $295.25 being made by the borrower on the note.
- **Interest.** This is the amount of interest being paid each month by the borrower. This amount decreases each month according to the amortization schedule for the thirty-year note.

- **Principal.** This is the amount of principal being paid each month by the borrower. This amount increases each month according to the amortization schedule for the thirty-year note.
- **Partial Payoff.** This keeps track of the principal balance of the partial each month. This amount decreases each month as the principal portion of each payment is applied. Observe how, in the beginning of the partial term, this amount is the full $15,000. As we approach payment number seventy-seven, the partial payoff is gradually reduced down to zero.
- **Note Balance.** This keeps track of the principal balance of the underlying 360-month loan, with respect to what is owed by the borrower making the payments.

If at some point during the partial term the note gets paid off early by the borrower, then the note servicer will refer to this schedule to determine the payoff amount as well as how to disburse the payoff funds.

We will suppose that in month fifty of the partial, the borrower pays off the loan in full.

- The note balance is $49,817.53, and this is the outstanding principal amount that the borrower will pay plus any additional daily accrued interest.
- The partial payoff is $6,813.13, which is the principal balance of the partial, and will be paid out to us as the owner of the partial.
- The difference between the note balance and the partial payoff is the amount of principal due to the holder of the underlying note. $49,817.15 - $6,813.13 = $43,004.02

What happened to the three parties involved in this transaction?

- The borrower was not impacted in any way. They continued along with the original terms of the note that they agreed to and signed when taking out the loan, which was to make thirty years of monthly payments at 5% interest in the amount of $295.25 per month. They paid off their loan early in month 292 of the amortization schedule with a principal balance of $49,817.13.
- The note owner (who was the seller of the partial to us) ended up collecting nineteen monthly payments of $295.25 from the borrower and then receiving $15,000 from us when they sold the partial.
- We (the buyer of the partial) ended up receiving fifty monthly payments of $295.25, a total of $14,762.50, of which $6,575.63 is interest and $8,186.87 is returned principal. Then we received the distribution of the partial payoff of $6,813.13. In total, we have received our $15,000 principal amount back as follows:

$8,186.87	Returned principal from monthly payments
+ $6,813.13	Partial payoff

$15,000.00	Initial investment amount
$6,575.63	Interest income or profit

KEY CONCEPTS

- Partials offer a high level of flexibility to both the buyer and seller by allowing a means to facilitate the purchase and sale of only part of a note or payment stream.
- Benefits to the buyer include participation in the owning of a note with a lower amount of capital investment, a means of partnership together with the partial seller, and having an aligned objective with respect to the continued success of the note investment.
- Benefits to the seller include flexibility in selling only the number of payments needed in order to raise a specific amount of needed capital while retaining the back end of the note and flexibility in being able to quickly raise liquid capital.
- The number of payments that are transacted in a partial can be just about anything that is agreed to between the seller and buyer.

13

NOTE FUNDS

INVESTING IN NOTE FUNDS AS A TRULY PASSIVE INVESTOR

The richest people in the world look for and build networks; everyone else looks for work.

—Robert Kiyosaki, bestselling author of Rich Dad Poor Dad

Investing in a note fund is an excellent option for investors who do not have the available time to dedicate to note investing, those who prefer a true passive investment, or those who do not yet have the experience to invest in notes on their own and wish to learn the business by observing first.

Some of the top benefits of note-fund investing:

- Allows investors to leverage the time, skills, experience, business relationships, and expertise of the fund managers
- Investors are able to realize the benefits of passive cash flow, earning a strong return on their capital
- Minimal liability exposure for investors
- Allows for diversification of the investment, spreading out risk over hundreds or thousands of assets in the fund, just like an insurance company will spread out their risk by writing many insurance policies
- Compliance and regulatory responsibilities are handled by the fund
- Ideal for self-directed accounts that require investors to maintain an arm's length from the ongoing operations of the investment

Note funds are much like real estate syndications in that they allow investors to pool their capital together in order to invest in larger assets than they could afford or manage on their own.

If an investor has $50,000 or $100,000 that they are looking to invest, they could possibly buy one or two notes with that amount of capital. All of that capital will be focused on the performance of one or two assets. However, if that capital were invested into a fund, it could be pooled together into a multimillion-dollar fund containing many assets, and the investor's risk is now spread out while minimizing the potential downside because the investor's position is not being determined by the outcome of one or two assets.

This is a rather simple structure between the fund sponsor and the investors. The fund sponsor/manager goes out and raises capital from investors. This capital is pooled together and then utilized to purchase notes in greater volume. Due to the larger transaction sizes of these purchases, the fund is able to benefit from acquisition of notes at a lower cost. The fund managers operate the fund and manage the note portfolio over time, increasing the value, and from the note income are able to pay a nice return to the investors of the fund.

Managing a large note portfolio involves a significant amount of heavy lifting: raising capital, investor relations, sourcing of notes, due diligence, asset management, and regulatory compliance. These responsibilities are all handled by the fund operators or principals.

Funds that are set up properly are set up using a private placement memorandum (commonly called a PPM) and have gone through the legal process to establish the fund with all the necessary SEC (Securities and Exchange Commission) filings.

There are note funds that operate using different business models and different operating structures, such as:

- Focus on performing notes
- Focus on defaulted notes
- Regional or geographic focus
- Focus on a particular property type

As a passive investor, when considering a fund, it is important to consider your own risk tolerance and to perform your due diligence on the fund and the key personnel managing the fund.

Here are some important questions to consider when evaluating a fund.

What is the experience and track record of the fund and the fund manager? This can be verified through checking business and personal references, running background checks on the individuals, verification of SEC (Securities and Exchange Commission) filings, and compliance at the federal and state levels.

What is the business model of the fund and its stated operational objective? Are you comfortable with the model, and do you have a clear understanding on how it will operate as an ongoing concern?

Is the fund open ended, or close ended, either by duration of time or by amount of capital raised?

When and how do investors get their capital returned?

What is the proposed arrangement for returns to be paid to investors? Are returns paid out immediately or deferred for a defined period of time? Is there a future event that kicks off payment of returns to investors? Do investors earn a fixed rate of return or a percentage of profits in the fund, or a combination of both?

Is the fund in good standing with the Better Business Bureau and the SEC (both at the state and federal levels)? Remember, always trust but verify firsthand.

Is the fund properly set up as an offering compliant with SEC regulations? We are extremely fortunate to have the SEC operating in an oversight capacity across the US. This helps the investment industry overall to protect the interests of investors and make sure that fund managers are providing good investment offerings to their investors.

WALKING IS FUN, BUT TAKING A RIDE CAN BE FASTER

Harold, a successful medical malpractice attorney with his own thriving boutique law practice, became very interested in investing in note funds. He had achieved many successes investing with partners in local commercial real estate projects over the years (interestingly enough, he liked investing in the niche asset class of medical office buildings); however, he was so busy with his law practice that he was finding it rather difficult to dedicate any time to finding new real estate opportunities. Harold was able to "take note of new opportunities" by investing in himself and becoming knowledgeable about investing in note funds. He found that, by investing in a note fund, it offered him a unique opportunity to invest passively and generate the cash flow income that he was seeking. He really liked the idea of being able to leverage the experience, expertise, and relationships of the fund manager. After just a few months of establishing a relationship and entering into a note fund investment, Harold was thrilled that he was receiving a cash flow stream of recurring income while continuing to focus his time and effort on growing his own business.

KEY CONCEPTS

- Investing in a note fund can be ideal for a busy investor who is interested in getting involved in note investing but does not have the time available to focus on the business.
- Note funds are structured similarly to real estate syndications in a manner that allows investors to pool their capital together in order to invest in larger assets than they could afford on their own, offering the benefits of economies of scale.
- An investor can realize tremendous diversification by investing in a note fund. Instead of deploying capital individually into only one or two notes, the investor is able to diversify risk by investing that same capital across hundreds or even thousands of notes.
- Participating in a note fund allows the investors to benefit from leveraging the time, skills, experience, business relationships, and expertise of the fund managers and principals.
- When evaluating a note fund, the due diligence on the investment opportunity is extremely important. The experience, track record, business model, payment arrangements, and SEC status are all important aspects that should be carefully evaluated and considered before investing.

14

HOW TO UTILIZE DEBT TO BUY AND PAY FOR THINGS THAT YOU MIGHT TYPICALLY BUY WITH DEBT

You have to move from just working for money
to a world where money works for you.

—Tony Robbins, American author, coach, and motivational speaker

In this chapter, we will explore the concept of investing in a performing note (or a note fund) and using the monthly income from the investment payments to make your secured debt payment.

A rather interesting concept is to make a large purchase using financing, and then turn around and buy debt so that you can use the monthly payments from that asset to service the debt on the financing that you have in place.

For example, let's say that you have about $27,000 in cash and that you are in the process of purchasing a car. You find a car you like, and it has an approximate price of $27,000.

You could certainly go ahead and purchase the car using that cash, and then you would not have any debt on the car. However, what if you financed the car with a car loan because the dealer was offering a nice financing incentive? We have all seen those auto advertisements where you could get financing at a very low rate in order to incentivize auto sales. Using our example, you walk into the dealer and buy the car, and take advantage of the financing offer, which comes with a special interest rate of 1.9% for borrowers that have excellent credit.

You go ahead and buy the car with the financing. Let's take a closer look at the terms of the financing offered by the dealer:

- Loan amount: $27,000
- Interest: 1.9%
- Loan term: 72 months
- Monthly payment: $397

Next, you are looking to buy a note with the cash you have, and you find a nice performing note for sale.

- Purchase price: $26,889
- Loan balance (UPB): $38,960
- Payment amount: $424.16
- Remaining payments: 116
- Rate of return on the note based on the above parameters: 14%

You then proceed to go ahead and buy that note. The end result is that you receive monthly payments of $424.16 each month, which you use to make your monthly auto payment of $397. You even have a little bit left over each month that can be used to top off the gas tank!

The concept that is illustrated in this example is known as "arbitrage," which is defined as the practice of taking advantage of a price difference between different markets in order to capitalize, or profit, on the difference. In this example, the arbitrage is coming from the difference between the rate we are lending on (14%) and the rate that we are borrowing at (1.9%).

I would like to draw your attention to the difference in term between the two notes—the car note has a 72-month term, and the note you bought has a 116-month term. The beauty is that once your car note has been fully paid off, you will still have 44 remaining monthly payments coming in!

This same concept can be utilized to take advantage by making payments on other low-cost debt, such as student loans and even your home mortgage debt. Further expanding on this concept, you are able to purchase as many multiple notes as you need in order to structure the cumulative monthly payment amount that you require in order to effectively implement this strategy.

FINAL THOUGHTS

Learning without implementation of the concepts learned and actually executing on them is quite useless. My sincere hope is that the topics, stories, and case studies that I have covered in this book will have opened your eyes to an amazing asset class and will inspire you to get started in the exciting world of note investing.

Why not set the intention right now to take note of new opportunities around you and take action? I encourage you to continue your education in note investing. If you decide that note investing is a good fit for you, then get involved in a way that suits your lifestyle—whether that means buying your first note(s) or investing in a note fund. Earlier in the book I highlighted the concept that note investing is a learning by doing business. Certainly it is very important that you spend time to get educated in the beginning as you are getting started, however, your education will continue to build as you get your feet wet and start actually investing and building your expertise.

I have seen firsthand numerous colleagues and friends undergo amazing personal transformations as a result of getting involved in note investing.

Alice—through note investing, she was able to take her two children's modest college savings fund of $150,000 and grow and compound it within five years to the point where she was able to easily pay for all their college expenses for their four years of undergraduate studies.

Mario—accepted a junior-level position working at a large note servicing company, having come into the role not knowing anything about the note investing industry. He ended up learning the back office side of the note business, as well as interacting with countless note investors and building powerful customer relationships throughout the course of his work. After a couple of years, he decided to take note of new opportunities and started buying individual mortgage notes for his own account. Mario eventually left that employer, going out on his own, and in the course of ten years he scaled his business massively, building a flourishing note business, which today routinely participates in multimillion-dollar transactions involving larger institutional note funds.

Ben—saw what was an amazing opportunity and decided to go full time into the note business, and went from earning $35,000 annually as an athletic fields groundskeeper to running his own flourishing note investing business within five years, where he was investing in notes for his own account as well as providing asset management services for other note investors. Before long, Ben realized that he was earning four to five times his old salary from his previous job. Later on, he was able to retire his wife from her full-time teaching job so that she could focus on raising their growing family.

Tim—was a veteran in the industry working in the mortgage loan origination business helping homeowners obtain mortgage loans for purchasing or refinancing their homes. With this background, he was quite familiar with notes and the secondary mortgage market, and he took note of new opportunities by investing $50,000 of his own capital into a successful note fund. This exposed him to the immense power of note investing as an asset class. After a few years of receiving consistent return payments, he became increasingly drawn toward the operational side of the note business and decided to join the note fund as a managing partner and operator of the fund. After a decade, that investment fund has steadily grown to be one of the major players in the note investing industry.

THAT'S THE POWER OF NOTE INVESTING.

Thank you for honoring me with the gift of your valuable time, which you have *invested* in reading this book. I look forward to hearing about your own success! Join me at FredMoskowitz.com and connect with me so that we can continue the conversation.

KNOWN AND UNKNOWN CONTRIBUTORS

Our best thoughts come from others.

—Ralph Waldo Emerson

KNOWN AND UNKNOWN CONTRIBUTORS

If your name appears here, you were directly responsible for at least one concept, one insight, one inspiration, or one experience together with me that has come together in the creation of this book.

Joshua Andrews

Tom Bertz

Tim Ferriss

Peter Fortunato

Seth Godin

Jeffrey Gitomer

Mark J. Kohler

Jeff Lazarus

Bill McCafferty

Jack Miller

Wendy Newdeck

Jimmy Napier

Bob Paulus

Simon Sinek

Martin Saenz

John Sweeney

Dave Van Horn

Zig Ziglar

ABOUT THE AUTHOR

ABOUT THE AUTHOR

Fred Moskowitz is an author, entrepreneur, and speaker who is on a personal mission to teach people about the power of investing in alternative asset classes, such as real estate and notes, showing them the way to diversify their capital into investments that are uncorrelated from Wall Street and the stock markets. Fred now publishes his concise yet definitive guide for new investors seeking to learn about the market niche of investing in residential mortgage notes. He's a frequent event speaker and contributor to investment podcasts and note industry conferences. You can visit him at FredMoskowitz.com.

The accumulated knowledge in this valuable book will greatly benefit those individuals who seek to achieve higher levels of financial freedom and develop expertise in the note investment arena.

Made in the USA
Coppell, TX
04 August 2024

35586764R00085